Advance praise for The Mission of Leadership

The words *hero*, *legend*, and *servant leader* are vastly overused in our world today, but they define General Shawn Campbell. I've had a ringside seat to observe him successfully leading immense organizations as well as taking the time and making the effort to inspire a middle school student. A leader is a leader all the time and in every situation. Within these pages, you will be exposed to time-tested, real-world principles that will impact you and those you serve.

　　—Jim Stovall, bestselling author of *The Ultimate Gift*

Shawn Campbell is a student, researcher, practitioner, and lifelong learner about leadership and its importance at work and in day-to-day life. *The Mission of Leadership* is a must-read as he's eloquently captured key concepts and lessons using real-world, practical examples. Shawn's style is easy to read with wide application for leaders at all levels, occupations, and stations in life!

　　—Brian T. Kelly, Lieutenant General, US Air
　　　　Force (Retired), and president and CEO of Military
　　　　　　Officers Association of America

Every aspiring, emerging, developing, and high-achieving leader seeks inputs and influences to cultivate, define, and achieve their success. Shawn Campbell offers an enlightening compilation of concepts, research, and experiences that will elevate leaders wherever they are in their journey. As a colleague and friend for more than two decades, I value his perspectives, thoughts, and counsel because I know he has already considered and very likely experienced the topic we're discussing. Shawn weaves impactful personal stories and lessons throughout his narrative, creating a useful digest for any stage of your career. As a reader (who's a leader), you will discover something new and useful every time you read *The Mission of Leadership*—it's an investment that pays off every time!

—**Colonel Paul Swenson,** US Air Force (Retired)

A delightful lesson in leadership from a seasoned and sage professional mentor who understands how to inspire and achieve the best from people, and oneself. There is a full measure of wisdom in each lesson.

—**Major General Troy Endicott,** US Space Force

The Mission of Leadership is a collection of leadership lessons, insights, and knowledge gained through experience leading at every level of an organization. Shawn is one of the most thoughtful leaders I know, and it comes across in this masterful piece. This resource should be added to every leader's library!

—**Jacob Werksman,** DBA, founder and CEO of Victory Strategies, executive fellow at Harvard Business School, and bestselling author of *Mastering Your G.A.P.: Unlocking the Leadership Power of Gravitas, Awareness, and Presence*

Brigadier General Shawn Campbell provides an experiential leadership anthology that thoughtfully shares his military experience from a servant-leader's perspective. This reflective and practical work both illustrates and examines leadership principles and is as useful for the first-line supervisor as it is helpful for the senior executive.

—**Ms. Patricia Mulcahy,** first-ever chief human capital officer, US Space Force

Just as he did when he served our nation, General Campbell hits yet another grand slam. A thought-provoking, educational, entertaining, and sobering view of hardcore leadership. From the successes to the failures, General Campbell clearly provides insight based not on theoretical beliefs but on real-world, critical, and demanding experiences. Every organization out there should have this on their reading list . . . it's that good!

—**Jerry P. Martinez,** Lieutenant General, US Air Force (Retired), and president and CEO, The TRAVTAY Group LLC

I have known Shawn only since early 2023, but that doesn't negate the impact he has had on my life and career. While I have had the honor of spending face-to-face time with him, many of you may not have that opportunity. Fortunately, as he's the man that he is, you now have the privilege of reading his words, which will transform your life and career the same way he did with mine and thousands of others around the world. No matter what your position in life, this is a book you will not want to miss!

—**Darren McKee,** founder of Darren McKee Co.

Superb read! Shawn delivers insightful nuggets to challenge every reader on their leadership journey with his genuine, practical approach based on his life story as a tremendously proven leader!

—**James Vechery,** Lieutenant General, US Air Force (Retired), and director of Mission Aviation Services Greensboro, Samaritan's Purse

Having served with Shawn Campbell, I've witnessed first-hand his uncanny ability to develop others. *The Mission of Leadership* captures that same presence. Reading it feels like sitting across from him, absorbing hard-won insights from a lifetime of leading. This isn't just a book; it's a coaching session that reminds us to apply the full spectrum of disciplines to maximize our impact on both the mission and our people. A must-read—and a must-use—for anyone serious about getting better at influencing others to maximize results while supporting teams.

—**Stephen T. Messenger,** DSL, founder of *The Maximum Standard*

I started reading Brigadier General Campbell's book and his story was so compelling that I read it in one sitting. Brigadier General Campbell is very candid about what he did well and what he learned and improved on. It takes a lot of courage to share mistakes that were made and how he successfully addressed them. I highly recommend this book to anyone interested in how to become an effective leader. Your time will be well spent!

—**Lieutenant General Gina Grosso,**
US Air Force (Retired)

When I was the director of logistics for US Central Command at the height of operations in both Iraq and Afghanistan, I needed the exact right leader to serve as my aide and executive officer; I hired Shawn. His superb skill sets—written and verbal communications, understanding and undertaking executive-level leadership vision and direction, being in the right place and time without fail, and keeping our staff on task and on target in high-demand, high-stakes environments—were second to none. We were blessed to have him on the team, making a daily difference, leading from the front, and always finding ways to take care of our team and our military families. Those same qualities leap off the pages of *The Mission of Leadership*.

—**Major General Ken Dowd,** US Army (Retired)

Shawn presents unique and practical leadership recommendations that will resonate with both new and seasoned leaders. As a senior leader in one of the world's largest organizations (the US military), he shares thoughts about preparing to lead, leadership strain, and overcoming failures that are particularly insightful and offer important guidance on how people can improve their leadership skills.

—**Alex Barelka, PhD, PMP,** professor of
management, Illinois State University

Having had the privilege of witnessing General Campbell lead airmen and guardians for more than twenty years, I've been consistently struck by his leadership style. He manages to be both deeply compassionate and laser-focused on the mission, a combination that genuinely makes people want to follow his lead. *The Mission of Leadership* feels like a natural extension of this approach, concentrating on three areas that have clearly been instrumental in his success: understanding your core values, leading with a clear drive for victory, and learning and growing from setbacks. What truly resonates is how he weaves in his own experiences, making the book feel less like a theoretical guide and more like a personal mentorship. Whether you're just starting out or have been navigating leadership roles for years, I believe you'll find his lessons incredibly impactful, truly important, and genuinely insightful—I know I certainly did.

—**Daniel R. Sitterly,** retired Senior Executive
Service and former assistant secretary,
Department of Veterans Affairs

The Mission of Leadership brings you into Shawn's world as a thirty-year leader in the US Air Force. He strikes a balance between tactical approaches and vulnerable stories that guide leaders toward a career of ongoing growth. Compelling, inspiring, and actionable for leaders across industries!

—**David Moerlein,** former Google leader and author of *The Safety Effect*

In *The Mission of Leadership*, General Campbell offers genuine, relatable leadership advice through a mix of failure and success stories. There's much clear, sage counsel here for leaders—whether aspiring or experienced, military or civilian. I continue to learn from this remarkable leader.

—**Brian Rendell,** Colonel, US Air Force (Retired), and senior director, Leadership Development, University of Texas at San Antonio

As leaders, we strive to embody a growth mindset and continually seek opportunities to learn and evolve. *The Mission of Leadership* wonderfully blends the humanity of leadership with a lifelong dedication of service to our nation, offering timeless truths and powerful insights that resonate across all sectors. General Campbell's experiences remind us that whether leading on the front lines, at the Pentagon, anywhere across a business, or in a corporate boardroom, the principles of effective leadership remain the same—and they are ones we must all embrace.

—**Timothy Eernisse,** vice president of Education and Growth and chief operating officer, National Educational Telecommunications Association

Shawn Campbell delivers a powerful and necessary message on what it truly means to lead well—and live well. With wisdom shaped by experience, he moves past the outdated idea of "work/life balance" and instead offers a framework of harmony between the professional and the personal. I've often thought of it as yin and yang—two interconnected forces that must coexist—and Shawn's insight captures that beautifully. His words are real, relatable, and deeply needed in today's leadership conversations. One line in particular captures the heart of this work: "A successful career isn't the rank with which you retire. It's a career for which the family you started with is still there with you at the end." This book doesn't just teach leadership—it honors life, legacy, and the people who matter most. I'm proud to support it and look forward to the impact it will have on leaders across every domain.

—**Brian Eddy,** Colonel, US Air Force (Retired), and founder and president, BondFire Ranch

Like many thought leaders, Shawn Campbell served and led with distinction. What makes his book *The Mission of Leadership* so compelling is Shawn's conversational tone and engaging writing style. He has many valuable insights to share and conveys them with clarity, vulnerability, and a self-deprecation that makes the reader want to listen. Shawn brings powerful perspectives earned through his rise from an enlisted member of the Air Force to his service as a general officer, a progression nearly impossible in today's military. His personal touches in these pages and encouragement to embrace failure resonate powerfully. I have already added this book to the required reading lists for my students and employees. What Shawn has created in these pages is a blueprint for success for new leaders but also a valuable "touchup" for experienced executives as they continue their leadership journeys. So, sharpen your axe, embrace some humility, and beware the dunking ducks!

—**Mark Anarumo, PhD,** retired permanent (full) professor and director of the Center for Character and Leadership Development at the US Air Force Academy and twenty-fourth president of Norwich University

Insightful, relatable and impactful! I have witnessed Shawn Campbell's positive impact firsthand from combat zones to corporate culture. Each chapter of *The Mission of Leadership* was like having a personal conversation over coffee with a friend and mentor, leaving you inspired to step up your game and apply the lessons to your own leadership situations!

—**Kyle Kremer,** Major General, US Air Force (Retired)

THE MISSION
OF LEADERSHIP

THE MISSION OF LEADERSHIP
The Character, Courage, and Conviction Leaders Need for Mission Success

ISBN: 978-1-964046-77-8
ISBN (hardback): 978-1-964046-84-6

DISCLAIMER: The views expressed are those of the authors and do not reflect the official guidance or position of the United States government, the Department of Defense, the United States Air Force, or the United States Space Force.

P

Expert Press
www.ExpertPress.net

Expert Press
11610 Pleasant Ridge Rd.
Suite 103, #189
Little Rock, AR 72223
www.ExpertPress.net

Editing by Michael Hume
Copyediting by Hannah Skaggs
Proofreading by Geena Barret
Text design and composition by Emily Fritz
Cover design by Casey Fritz

THE MISSION OF LEADERSHIP

THE CHARACTER, COURAGE, AND CONVICTION LEADERS NEED FOR MISSION SUCCESS

SHAWN W. CAMPBELL

Brigadier General, US Air Force (Retired)

This is first and foremost dedicated to my best friend and bride, who encouraged me to share these sentiments and stories, and to our children, who were first-row action figures in this life and who inspired me to be the very best I could be.

This is also dedicated to the amazing and accomplished leaders, many of whom are referenced in this book, who engaged, energized, and encouraged me to become a better leader in life, not just in the Air Force, and one who would make a difference.

Finally, this is dedicated to my family, friends, and followers who believed in me.

—Shawn

Then I heard the voice of the Lord saying,
"Whom shall I send? And who will go for us?"
And I said, "Here am I. Send me!"
—Isaiah 6:8 (English Standard Version)

CONTENTS

FOREWORD

In December 2019, President Donald Trump signed the 2020 National Defense Authorization Act establishing the United States Space Force and signed another document that appointed me as the first chief of Space Operations and the first, and only, Space Force Guardian.

It was daunting to think of the task ahead in establishing a new armed service inside the Department of Defense, which hadn't been done in seventy-two years, since the Air Force separated from the United States Army back in 1947.

As an "army of one," I knew my priority was to grow the force and to create a service custom-built for space and for the twenty-first century. That was going to take top-tier leadership talent. My first hires were Ms. Pat Mulcahy, a recognized transformational personnel leader, and Brigadier General Shawn Campbell, a career personnel leader in the United States Air Force, as her deputy.

I outlined two big risks that we faced: first, not thinking boldly enough to build the Space Force our national security demanded, and second, when we did think boldly, being squashed by the bureaucracy because that is not how we have done business in the past. Over the course of the new service's establishment, we had to contend with both risks.

Leadership is tested in times of transition and transformation. We needed leaders who were not only grounded in purpose but bold enough to chart new paths. Brigadier General Campbell was exactly that kind of leader. I had the privilege of observing his leadership during an extraordinary time of change. He brought clarity, creativity, and a sense of calmness under pressure as we moved out with alacrity to build this new service from the ground up.

His vision in developing the Space Force's groundbreaking human capital strategy shaped policies and programs not just for the Space Force but as disruptive examples for the entire Department of Defense, and it continues to define how we attract, develop, retain, and lead today's military and civilian guardians.

In this book, you will see his leadership principles in action organized in three powerful sections: "True North," "Leading for Victory," and "Failure Is Not Defeat." Each of these sections contains chapters full of real-life leadership examples gleaned over a long and distinguished Air Force career—a career spent making tough decisions, leading and developing people, and staying calm and cool under intense pressure.

Whether writing about the importance of having a guiding purpose (a "North Star"), or the value of teaching and trusting your team, or how to learn from failure, the theme is consistent: Great leadership is both principled and practiced.

I recommend this book to anyone who aspires to lead with courage and conviction—whether you're just starting your leadership journey or have decades of experience behind you. Brigadier General (Retired) Shawn Campbell is a transformative leader, and the lessons in these pages reflect both his character and his commitment to serving and leading well.

Let this book help guide you on your leadership journey. Find your North Star—and lead boldly.

John W. "Jay" Raymond
General (Retired), United States Space Force
First chief of Space Operations

INTRODUCTION
PURPOSE AND POLARIS

Do something wonderful, people may imitate it.
—Albert Schweitzer

It was January 2020, and I was on my way from Washington, DC, to the US Air Force Academy in Colorado for a few days. I needed to do some specific work progressing a number of programs for the Air Force Office of Talent Management Innovation, the unit at the Pentagon I was leading at the time.

I arrived at the Dallas-Fort Worth airport, and just before it was time to catch my connecting flight to Colorado Springs, my cell phone rang. I didn't recognize the number, but I saw that it had a 202 area code—Washington, DC. I don't often answer calls from unfamiliar phone numbers, but that still, small voice inside told me I needed to answer this one.

It was Ms. Patricia Mulcahy, a Senior Executive Service leader in the Department of the Air Force—the civilian equivalent of a general officer who outranked me quite considerably at that time. I hadn't known her for very long.

She asked me if I would consider becoming her deputy.

What she was asking me to do was to become the first-ever deputy chief human capital officer for the newly formed United States Space Force, which had been signed into law as the first new American military service in more than seventy years a few weeks prior to this phone call.

My first thought? *That sounds cool! We're going to do something truly historic. Yeah, I want to be a part of that.*

Another part of me said, *This sounds like an awful lot of work. I don't know if I can rise to this challenge.*

Ms. Mulcahy and I had a brief conversation, which I understood was not really an interview. It was more of a sensing session to explore my thinking about this opportunity.

"Have you spoken with Lieutenant General Brian Kelly?" I asked. "If he supports it, then yes, I'm in." (I'll introduce General Kelly in more detail later. He was my boss at the time.) I promised to call her back when I got settled in Colorado Springs a couple of hours later to make sure that everything had come together.

As I hung up the phone, it occurred to me that her conversation with General Kelly had probably already happened; again, while I hadn't known Ms. Mulcahy for very long, I knew her well enough to know that she had already done due diligence and had already thought deliberately and deeply about asking me to join her on this adventure. What she was saying was more like "General Kelly and I agree this is the best course of action for both the Air and Space Forces." I was not being "cordially invited"—more like "cordially assigned." We are very rarely able to choose our exact assignments, and at that point in my career, as an executive-level leader, I had long been committed to going all in. Wherever I was most needed, that was where I was going to go. Being asked to do this, knowing others could have been selected who may well have been better at it than I would, was a great honor. When I called Ms. Mulcahy back, she shared that everything had indeed been discussed and that we were ready to move forward.

My current team and I were working on a number of ongoing projects, and I felt as though I owed it to them and to General Kelly to wrap up some of those things and put them in a good place for my successor, who wouldn't be arriving until six months later. Ms. Mulcahy asked me to consider heading back to the Pentagon to start the new job immediately given all we had before us and the time demands, but we ended up negotiating a start date in May 2020.

However, on March 15 of that year, the staff were instructed to depart the Pentagon en masse—COVID-19 pandemic-related actions and activities had begun. We were just beginning to understand what was happening and to make decisions about normal operations going forward.

Beyond "normal operations," our team was about to build the first new United States military service in decades, and we would have to do it during a time of unbelievable stress and duress because of this once-in-a-century, unpredicted, and unprecedented pandemic.

In the early days of the pandemic, we didn't know what we didn't know. What we did know was that we were building the new Space Force in a digitally distributed way—most of the teammates weren't at the Pentagon, where we normally would have been planning together and doing the deliberate, deep work of building the service. It was a time of super stress and chaotic challenge.

It was also a time of amazing vision and value. It took great vision to build something entirely new, to take the US Space Force in a direction that none of the other services had been able to move with speed and deliberateness. (That's neither good nor bad—because it's a bureaucratic machine, it's just the reality that things don't usually move quickly.)

General John "Jay" Raymond, the first chief of Space Operations, (who wrote the foreword to this book) often said, "We have a clean sheet. We have an open field in which to run. We can set this up the way we want it to be." He gave us a great North Star to guide our work: We would proceed with purpose and passion even though the circumstances were uncertain.

That's one of the reasons this book is important to me. Throughout my journey as a leader, both inside the Air Force and following my military service retirement, I have long realized and recognized that having that North Star, a guiding path and purpose, is irreducibly important to the work we undertake as leaders.

At the very beginning of my time in the Air Force, I wasn't serving to learn leadership; rather, it was simply a means to an end. I was a junior in college and was looking for a way to finish paying for my undergraduate education. My roommate at the time was in the US Navy. Based on a number of conversations with him, the military seemed a good and logical opportunity to learn a skill, pay the bills, and fund my degree using GI Bill benefits. I never intended to spend a full career with the Air Force. Though it wound up being thirty years, two months, and eight days of active duty, my original intention was to complete my four-year contract, go home, finish those undergraduate studies, and go into the corporate world. I thought I might become a business executive at some point in my career, but a different North Star was presented, and it lit my path. My dedication included a passage from the biblical Old Testament book Isaiah. Those words have long resonated with me, and part of why I served in the Air Force for as long as I did was because I thought it was my calling. It was where the North Star was brightly shining. My favorite picture in the Pentagon, of the many thousands adorning the hallways, depicts an Air Force pilot praying with his family in a church or chapel. That passage I shared from Isaiah is on the brass plate affixed to it.

Polaris is the astronomical name for what we know as the North Star. It's the star ancient mariners relied upon for direction, and as a metaphor, a professional's Polaris gives them direction and purpose. I understood relatively early in my career, when I came to both acknowledge and appreciate that the Air Force was my calling, my *mission*, that my entire purpose—my personal Polaris—was to become the best leader I could be inside the Air Force, which was giving me opportunity after opportunity to lead people in an organization where our mission mightily mattered.

I frankly fell in love with the idea of serving my nation, wearing the uniform, and learning to be the best leader I could be. It wasn't about being aggrandized or accumulating power or position. It was about fulfilling the mission that was given to me, in the fullness of its purpose, to accomplish whatever was necessary for our national security and defense.

Returning to the Albert Schweitzer quote above, my Polaris became a strong desire to do something wonderful so that others might imitate it. Learning to become an effective and infectious leader was a wonderful journey for me, and *The Mission of Leadership* is part of my effort to share what I've lived and learned on that journey (so far) so that others might find things they want to imitate during their own wonderful leadership journeys.

In Part I, we'll thoroughly discuss this idea of true north, which is so vital to a leader's success. Part II explores the different ways I've learned that leaders can lead their teams to victory, however victory might be defined by a given leader or organization. Finally, Part III describes the power of using the inevitable failures all leaders face to learn more and become even more impactful.

Ready to go? Turn the page, and let's start this mission together.

PART I
YOUR TRUE NORTH

I don't know what your destiny will be,
but one thing I do know:
The only ones among you who will be really happy
are those who will have sought and found a way to serve.
—Albert Schweitzer

x

CHAPTER 1
ALL THRUST, NO VECTOR

Give me six hours to chop down a tree,
and I will spend the first four sharpening the axe.
—Abraham Lincoln

Leadership is a verb. It requires applied action and attention. A leader must move and motivate others to move. Leadership also starts with deliberate decisions and purposeful planning. Like sharpening the axe in Lincoln's quote above, it is taking the time to properly prepare to accomplish the roles, responsibilities, and requirements we either have now or will take over later. That planning doesn't need to be fully detailed at the outset, but a leader needs to be thoughtful about how they're going to approach each post or position.

Borrowing from flight principles, thrust is what airplane engines provide to overcome inertia and take to the air. Vector is a specific direction or destination to which we're flying. As a leader, I couldn't just take off. I had to understand to where I intended to travel.

For me, the planning typically started with addressing a few key questions:

- What's the mission of the organization I'm going into?
- What are the organizational objectives for which I'm going to be responsible, either for supporting or for delivering wholesale?
- What do I need to do, or deliberately think through, before I even get there?

I think leaders sometimes just assume, *Well, I'll figure it out when I get there. I'll spend the first thirty or sixty or ninety days getting to know the people, getting to know the organization.* By contrast, The Ohio State University, among others, defines a kind of forward planning as *initiating structure.* Initiating structure, or initiating action, as the term implies, means that starting the reading, researching, relating to, and understanding of things at some level of detail must occur as early as possible. Weeks or months after starting the new leadership position is too late.

The practice that I undertook for many years was to set scheduled times—once a week, once every other week, or even once a month—to "sharpen my axe" by spending time with the incumbent I'd be replacing. This way, I could start to understand from their perspective what was happening in the organization and what I would need to know before I assumed the position.

These were often digging into simple things, such as the current organizational chart (although some personnel would likely change before I was on board, it helped me understand how the operation was orchestrated or oriented) and key items on which the current leadership team was working. By seeing them ahead of time, I could start to get my mind around them.

These meetings often led to additional research and reading. Then, when I got into the position, I wasn't spending time learning things every single day that I could have, or, more pointedly, should have learned before I got there.

In some respects, it's like being a professional athlete, or an athlete at any level: We practice before getting to the game. This was my way of thinking and preparing to take on the new role. I didn't have to have everything fully "baked," but I needed to start to understand the team and its goals. Then it was time to start framing how I would adapt to the needs of the organization, as opposed to expecting the organization to understand my personal leadership vision and style and bend to it.

ADAPTING YOUR LEADERSHIP UNIVERSALS

There are things that are universal in leadership, some of which we'll talk about in other parts of the book, but really these are just fundamental truisms in leadership and applicable anywhere. There are things that need to be adopted and adapted to the specific role you're about to go into, at any layer or level in an organization.

For example, in an organization that's already high-performing, there are things we're probably going to do more around the edges to buttress and build on that performance, as opposed to what we would do in an organization that has significant challenges or is even failing. Knowing which type of "game" we're going into affects the way we prepare for that game. It's not just about taking this universal approach of saying, "Here's the way I think about leadership" and then fitting the organization to my leadership style. It's more like asking myself, *How do I adapt my anchor points as a leader so they best help to generate the successes and objective outcomes we're trying to achieve in this organization?*

Again, it's about being thoughtful, deliberate, and detailed in planning before we get into the position. When we arrive, yes, we're going to meet most of the people for the first time. Yes, we're now in full contact with what's happening in the organization. But coming in with that thoughtful preparation really helps speed and support successful leadership there.

When I assumed my first Colonel command at Scott Air Force Base in Illinois, what the US Air Force considers the first executive-level position, I wanted to know everything about the base before I even got there. I'd been there a couple times for a few days for meetings but never worked there. Before arriving, I deliberately learned basic things like that thirty-two different organizations are represented on the installation, 3,500 acres comprise the landmass for which I would now be responsible for maintaining safety and security (including police and fire protective services), and I'd need to make sure there were no bad actors on the installation.

I also needed to understand the dynamics of many other factors, such as these:

- How many people am I leading, serving, and supporting?
- How many dollars and other assets do we have to work with?
- What do the higher headquarters need for the organization to deliver?

I learned everything I could before I assumed my command. I learned I would be leading 1,520 people directly and supporting approximately another 12,000 as customers and consumers of our services. I learned how many facilities were on the installation, all of which the team I was leading would be maintaining: 868 buildings, not counting base housing, which added another 1,525 facilities. I learned how many roads we would have to maintain: 76 paved miles. I knew that the oldest building on the installation was built in 1920. I learned about the century-long history of the base. It wasn't just about the facts and figures, the scope and scale; it was about getting my mind around the organization and understanding my team's role in daily flying missions, among others on the base. For example, when I met with the public works leader, a civil engineer, I already knew a lot of these things. Not that they didn't matter, but we could move past the basic details and into the depth of things I needed to learn, like the number of repair, renovation, or construction projects in progress or planned, the real priorities, and my responsibilities to deliver them.

As leaders, it's really about doing the "reps and sets," preparing ourselves, and getting ready to blend what needs to be done with authenticity in who we are as leaders. It's not about just walking around and saying "I'm the guy in charge! You'll do the things I'm directing you to do!" There's a big difference between that and an approach based on having actual knowledge of how the organization operates and adapting our leadership abilities to find and focus on areas of potential improvement.

Many leaders won't be in their positions for very long. Not just in the military, but even in Fortune 500 companies, it's not unusual for executives to be in their positions for just a few years or less. They get promoted or take an opportunity in another organization. Leading shouldn't be about leaving my mark but about figuring out how to make sure the organization is most successful. A leader has to give deliberate thought to it, plan for desired outcomes, and get into data and detail.

I didn't get it right all the time. There were times when I was "all thrust, no vector." I just pushed as hard and fast as

I could without carefully considering where I was supposed to successfully land. I certainly made mistakes in leadership positions, such as making decisions when I thought I had the most useful or relevant information only to find out later that it was incorrect. One example is understanding how I presented myself to those I was directly leading and those whom I may well be influencing, good or bad, by how I operated. As a young officer, at this point a Captain, starting a new leadership role at Spangdahlem Air Base in Germany, I wanted to make a quick impression. So I did what I'd seen many other leaders do: I added a tagline, or "bumper sticker" to my email signature block: "Work hard, Demand excellence, Expect results."

My thinking was that this would help my teammates understand my perspectives pertaining to our work. They would expect me to display and demonstrate these attributes, my desire would be obvious to them, and they would follow suit. I was wrong, in a number of ways. The words I chose were all thrust, no vector. What did those three grouped actions actually look like in application? What were the measured outcomes of success? What were the data and details I would be reviewing or viewing to give those I was leading a clear understanding of what "good" or "right" looked like?

Also, choosing to use *demand* and *expect* at first seemed like I was simply setting a high bar, but it came across as authoritative and autocratic. Some shared with me that they thought I was setting impossible standards precisely because there were no provided metrics or messaging about what standards we were actually trying to set. Lots of thrust! Go, do, act. But no vector.

Not only did I rethink these word choices but I also removed them from my tagline and, by and large, from my leadership lexicon. They weren't bad ideas in and of themselves. After all, we were a results-driven organization, and one of the Air Force's core values is "Excellence in all we do." It was the specific, or specious (depending on the receiver), lack of clarity and connection to outcomes that left some, if not many, of those around me with the blast of thrust only.

I hadn't been deliberate enough in setting my vector. I hadn't deliberately gone through the steps I needed to go through as the leader. I had to recognize my responsibility to tell people what I needed or wanted them to do and not just assume they understood.

It's incumbent on leaders, no matter where we are in the organization—at the front end or in the executive suite—to be thoughtful about the details and take a deliberate approach to what we do. This isn't just, to borrow a phrase from the Air Force, "flying by the seat of your pants." Just as pilots undertake specific mission planning, including plotting the pathway to their destination and back, the best leaders develop, deploy, and deliver deliberate plans focused on meeting and maintaining key objectives and outcomes.

IT's PERSONAL, TOO

That was one example of my failure to fully understand the environment and how my actions, however well intended, necessitated more deliberateness. It also highlighted the fact that leadership isn't time-bound, meaning a little more effort prior to departing the office one day was all I would have needed to address and adjust my email tagline.

It can be very easy to be all-consumed with our work, particularly in a leadership position. I grew up with the context that leadership is 24/7/365, not Monday through Friday, nine-to-five. I don't mean this as a slight, but for me, leadership was not like "banking hours," when I can go in and engage a teller personally to transact my business. It's very easy to slip or slide into this idea that it's necessary to be "on" all the time. And I often got that wrong.

Across my career, my greatest partner was my wife. We have been together for the entirety of my Air Force career, dating before I entered Air Force service and married a year after. She was there for every bit of it and couldn't have been more supportive. I would call her and say, "Hey, this is what's happening at the office, this is what I'm working on," and she would simply respond, "Do what you need to do."

My wife wasn't saying, "Ignore all your responsibilities as a husband or a father," though. This is why I say sometimes I got this balance wrong. My caution and recommendation to leaders is to be very thoughtful about calibrating this. It is entirely possible, and preferable, to reach our professional goals without making our careers the be-all, end-all of our lives. I know many super-successful executives, including generals and admirals, who modeled and maintained a better balance than I did.

For many years, I've heard of this notion of trying to find "work/life balance." I've read a lot of relevant research about it, which has indicated it's a fallacy. What we're really talking about is *harmonizing* the two parts of who we are: our personal lives and our professional lives.

There are going to be days in leadership (particularly as an executive) that are all-consuming. We're going to be doing twelve-, fourteen-, maybe even eighteen-hour days at work now and then, depending on what's happening. We might have a hot project or a big program that's getting ready to be launched. In a military context, operations our team is about to undertake may require longer working days.

But that's not every day. Again, it's easy to slip into a mode in which we tell ourselves to push up fourteen, fifteen, or sixteen hours every day. We go home, eat, kiss the wife, kiss the kids, and go to bed, then just "wash, rinse, repeat" the next day. Instead, a good leader needs to recognize that harmonizing life looks like this: Monday might be a sixteen-hour day, but Tuesday perhaps I'm done at two o'clock in the afternoon and I don't need to stay on the job for another five to seven hours. Maybe my son has a concert that afternoon or early evening, or maybe my daughter has a play that I really need to attend. We need to give ourselves permission as leaders to remember that the work will still be there after we attend to our family's needs or wants. We need to say to ourselves, *I'm meeting my obligations and responsibilities at work, and it's okay for me to take an afternoon off to do something that's important to my family.*

Again, I have to be clear: I got this out of balance for most of my career. I was often more focused on the professional than on the personal. I eventually listened to those around me and began giving myself permission to harmonize much better. At the end of it, a successful career isn't the rank with which you retire. It's a career for which the family we started with is still there with us at the end. The trappings of position and authority and opportunities are great, but we want to, and absolutely can, successfully navigate our careers all the way to the executive level so that the people who are most important to us are still with us at the end of the career, as we close one chapter and open another.

Setting the Vector

This is why the idea of setting our professional mission, vision, and objectives is so important. A notable number of mentors and professionals I've followed say it's best to write down the things we want to accomplish. Taking time to put pen on paper or type things out is not so much about having a checklist of things to be marked off as it is about having a way to order our thoughts about what we're about to do as leaders.

"Do I have a clear sense of my mission in this job? Do I have a vision, so that the people I'm leading can catch on to what I'm trying to do, something that's not just aspirational or inspirational but also directional—so those I lead know what I want to accomplish? How do I best move and motivate teammates here to be successful?"

Then it's a matter of identifying the objectives needing to be completed in order to meet the mission and vision.

I didn't do this for the first four years or so that I wore the uniform, but I got much more deliberate about it as a Captain and through the rest of my career. I sat down, gave deliberate thought to it, and eventually wrote out those objectives in advance, and in such detail that I was including the finer points by name: Who are the people at that assignment that I need to meet in the first seven, fourteen, or thirty days? Not just my boss or my peers, but also the "power players" around the organization who actually get things done. I wanted to be deliberate about taking time to go see those people, not beckoning them to my office if they were subordinate to me but actually going to their work centers, meeting them where they were, getting to know them, and starting to build those relationships.

I wrote down the names of those people by office, if I knew by looking at the organizational chart who they were in each position. Similarly, I wrote down the things I mentioned above: How many people, how many programs, how many facilities? What are the finances and other things for which I'm responsible? I wanted to write everything down so I could understand how each person or thing mattered to the position I was going into.

This practice helped me set overall objectives for each assignment. They weren't carved in stone. I knew things were going to change based on operational realities and day-to-day events, and that events were going to occur outside our ability to influence or inform some of that trajectory. But it was immensely helpful to just be thoughtful about it and to have a road map and game plan that mattered and could be shared with people. I shared that road map very openly.

I thus had what for many years I called the "top view," even before I went into a new assignment. It was a clear view of my key thoughts from the outset, typically a single page—a summary, not a detailed master plan. I shared it with my supervisor, my peers, and the people I was leading so that everyone knew what I was thinking and how I was approaching leadership in these different organizations. In some cases, things I had written down weren't as clear as I'd thought. I opened an opportunity not to challenge my thrust, but more to course-correct and adjust the vector or the plans.

Great leaders invite that kind of feedback. It's not about having some sort of Napoleonic complex of "I'm the person in charge, and this is my plan." No, I encouraged feedback. I wanted to hear things like "This is where we think you have it right, or about right."

"Here are some adjustments we might recommend."

"Here are some things we don't see in your top view, and here's why it matters."

Earlier in my Air Force career, I was invited to give advice to one of my colleagues who was going out to squadron command. This is the most important leadership level inside the United States Air Force because the squadron commander has the most direct, and therefore outsized, impact on people. A typical squadron is composed of a couple hundred to many hundreds of people. Air Force statistics indicate that people are more likely to either be retained or seek to depart military service based on their experience with the squadron commander (or equivalent leadership level, as I think this statistical indication holds true for all the service branches). This frontline unit leader has an enormous responsibility and enormous impact, not only on the men and women who wear the uniform but also on the civilians who serve.

My colleague had come to three of their peers (including me), asking our opinion about when a leader in that key position should have their first meeting with their teammates once they've taken the position. "What's the appropriate timing for me to sit down with my core leadership team and lay out things like mission, vision, objectives, my philosophy, and the things I'm thinking about?"

This new leader's formal command ceremony (an official military event) took place on a Friday, and all three of us recommended that they wait until Monday to sit down with the team and simply get to know them. We advised them to make that first meeting not about all their objectives for the next two to three years, or their grand mission and vision, but about taking an opportunity to meet people. For example, "Hi, my name is Shawn. You're Joe, or Jane, and here's what I know about you (because I've already done my homework, planned, and prepared). Tell me about your unit. Tell me about your family. Tell me about how you're leading in this organization. What's working? What do you need help with to make it work better?"

Yes, we should have done our deliberate planning, but we shouldn't use it as a cudgel as soon as we come into the position. Rather, once you get to know people, you can share your top view up front (holding back on any longer, more detailed document) and solicit feedback to tweak, press, reframe, or repackage it so that it makes the most sense. Again, I'm not saying I want my new team to "bend me to their will." I'm inviting a more open conversation about how to make the plan work best for our organization because we all want to be successful.

Based on our advice, our colleague changed their mind and decided not to have their first meeting that Friday, right after the command ceremony. As is customary, in the reception after the ceremony, the new commander shakes hands, meets and greets people, and afterward, they usually go into their office and start getting everything ready to dive into their new responsibilities. In this case, we assumed the first sit-down with the team would take place on Monday, based on the advice we'd given.

A number of months later, the three of us met again at a conference and noticed our colleague wasn't there. We learned that person had decided to have the first sit-down on Sunday morning, which is a bit of a problem. It's true that military members' schedules are very flexible and that we can be called in at any time of any day. Weekends aren't necessarily out-of-bounds when outside the normal schedule. But, civilian teammates can't be forced to come in at an unscheduled time; Sunday morning would not be a normal part of their schedule, with some position-specific exceptions. Unsurprisingly, about a third of our colleague's new leadership team did not come to that Sunday meeting, and this person reacted in exactly the wrong way. They sought to take administrative action against people, mostly civilians, who hadn't attended.

That's not all. Normally that first sit-down should be no more than one hour (as should most other meetings). I worked to make sure my staff meetings were less than one hour and were more about decision-making than just sharing information. But our colleague's first meeting lasted about four hours. Talk about all thrust, no vector! From the very beginning of their new leadership opportunity, this person, who was so well intended, alienated a bunch of the leaders they needed and would have to rely on to be successful. We were not surprised to learn that person had been removed from the position in part because they had started in exactly the wrong way. The old adage "You never get a second chance to make a first impression" certainly applied here. In leadership, there are few options or opportunities for a do-over, thus the need to plan for actions, activities, and ways to address teammates from the outset. Find and fixate on your vector, then apply thrust.

YOUR LEADERSHIP CONSTITUTION

The events we just reviewed happened in the first third of my career and helped me crystallize this idea of "all thrust, no vector." Our colleague hadn't thoughtfully planned things out, and consequently created a problem for themselves and unnecessary turbulence in the organization just because of how they had attempted to immerse themselves in their new position.

It helped me learn that we need to create for ourselves a good "leadership constitution" document, something we've thought very deliberately about. This document is a framework for the way I'm going to operate based on the things that are important to me as a leader and considerably connected to this organization. The Constitution of the United States is the framework for our three coequal branches of government and how they operate the federal system of governance for the country. Our framers were very thoughtful about doing their research; they looked at historical documents and considered ideas that did or didn't work well.

In crafting a leadership constitution, the idea is to create a framework for our own leadership principles and precepts to share with the teammates we're leading. That's not to say it can't be very well drawn out. It can be our own personal leadership guidebook or it could be as simple as one page in which we lay out the basic elements to focus on what we're trying to advance and accomplish.

In appendix A, you'll find a product I put together many, many years ago. When I went into leadership positions, I had a simple one-page chart that I shared with the team, and I always called it "Campbell's Cuts." I came to understand this collection as the basis for my leadership constitution many years later when I worked with a friend, Colonel Stephen Messenger, who holds a doctorate in strategic leadership and is an incredibly bright Army Colonel whom I had the opportunity to work with at US Transportation Command.

He impressed on me this idea of a leadership constitution, and here's what I love about this experience. Technically, I was his superior officer. I was a "full bird" Colonel, and he was a Lieutenant Colonel at the time. (Stephen's now a full-bird Colonel, still serving and teaching leadership at the US Army War College.) He had something to teach me, and that's something else I learned: We can learn from anybody. It doesn't have to be somebody that we would consider superior to us or more experienced.

Here, I listened to somebody who had a great idea, regardless of rank or position. In doing so, I found something that came to matter to me: an understanding of a strong leadership constitution. It outlines the answers to questions like these:

- What are the principles I'm living by?
- What matters to me as a leader?
- How do I view the way I'm supposed to execute my job?
- What are the basic parameters around me as a leader?
- What helps me understand what true north is for me?
- What am I going to focus on every day?

In my leadership constitution, some of those things exist in a military context, such as "Readiness is job one." We have a responsibility to protect and defend the Constitution of the United States, and that might mean going into physical combat. We did in the course of my career, and though I was never in direct combat, I understood that I was a force supporter and supplier to that effort. At any rate, the readiness imperative became part of my personal leadership constitution, and people knew it was a focus under my leadership.

This was an example of the things that I wanted people to know to which I would hold myself accountable. For me, being ready means being physically, mentally, spiritually, and socially prepared to do the things the nation might ask me to do. And I expected the same of the people around me. That's why that item is listed first in Campbell's Cuts. We need to be worthy every day.

Particularly in my last three or four promotions during my Air Force career, I talked a lot about the fact that I was only borrowing my new rank, for a time, from the nation I served. That was really important to me. I tried not just to live and lead with humility but to recognize that I had to put in the work to re-earn that rank every day, even as a Brigadier General, a C-suite leader.

Another article in my leadership constitution was catching people doing things well. It's easy to point out things that aren't going well, but how much time do I put into finding people doing things well? I would often say that investing in people is really important, if not the most important thing a leader does. That includes getting to know our people, even though we can't know every single excruciating detail about them. As we move up the leadership ladder, particularly in executive ranks where we may have thousands of people working for us, it's hard to get to know everybody. But I wanted every person I came into contact with to feel like I was doing just that—and not just for show. It was important to me to ask good questions.

We often just ask, "How are you doing today?" and the answer we often get is "I'm doing great." That's transactional. It's not without its usefulness, but contrast that typical transaction with a question like "What's been the best part of your day?" or "Tell me the best thing that happened to you today." That's a different concept, a different question, and it generates a very different answer. Now you're generating an opportunity for an investment in people, which, as a leader, can develop your relationship with that human a little bit more.

This brings up another constitutional element. How do people communicate? Am I communicating with "positive inquiry?" Are my questions likely to elicit more than a binary yes/no answer? Am I trying to get more out of that conversation, however brief?

Another thing that was really important to me was trying to be a fire preventer, not a firefighter. I wanted get ahead of things that could go wrong or go badly and work on them before they could become big problems.

Another element leaders talk about all the time is the "team concept." This is a very important aspect of my own leadership constitution, but my approach was to work to create an environment where people truly felt they could talk to me and give me feedback. I wanted to acknowledge that I was going to make mistakes (I've described one of my mistakes already) and that it was okay. I was only going to get better, not just by learning from my mistakes but by inviting and generating feedback from others, even if my mistakes weren't necessarily big ones. I wanted people to know it was okay to connect with me and share things that they had seen but that I might not have.

This is exactly how I learned, during my first Colonel command, my first executive role, that I was wearing my uniform incorrectly, and I hadn't even realized it. My ribbons were improperly displayed on my dress uniform (the military "business suit" complete with accoutrements). My official photo was taken while I was wearing that incorrectly configured uniform, and that picture was then placed on the wall in dozens of facilities across the base.

This is a big deal in the military. No one is going to criticize, or perhaps even notice, that a CEO is wearing a tie that doesn't beautifully or best match their shirt. But in the military services, since there is an absolute insistence on proper uniform wear at all levels and ranks, people will notice if ribbons are incorrectly or improperly worn.

As it turns out, a young officer, a Captain, came to see me because they had clear confidence that I meant what I had said about telling me things, including giving me corrective feedback. I had made it clear that anyone could call me out if something wasn't right or could be improved. This gave the Captain comfort about telling me that my uniform was incorrectly configured.

I fixed it. We had to retake the photo, and when those updated photos were distributed, I owned my mistake. I shared with the leadership team and many others around the organization that the reason we were updating the photo wasn't because I thought my smile wasn't good or my hair could've looked better. It was because my uniform was improper, and as a leader, getting the details right matters. I made a mistake, somebody corrected me, and I appreciated the feedback. We fixed it and moved on.

This uniform example connects to another point that's part of my leadership thinking. This goes to the notable notion of the team concept. A military uniform includes a tag that identifies the member's branch of service, such as "US Air Force," "US Army," and so forth (or insignia that simply displays "US"). I often pointed out to my teams that the very uniform they wear says "US." It doesn't say "ME," and some uniform configurations and circumstances don't include rank. Uniforms also don't indicate "I'm the person in the leadership position." Again, they show "US." Therefore, we are a team—first, last, and only. We are not an ungrouped, unaligned set of individuals. I believe that. I'm in a leadership position, but I'm most importantly your teammate.

One more element of my leadership constitution is an inverted pyramid as a way to think about organizational structure. Most organizations are hierarchical, depicted as a pyramid with somebody at the top and authority cascading downward from there. I tried to think of that structure as inverted and my primary responsibility, no matter where I was on the chart, as making everyone else in the organization successful. When you flip the pyramid upside-down, the most important people in the organization move to the top. It's the people on the front line who are doing the day-to-day activities that make the organization successful. If I'm going to be successful in a mission or vision, it will be by relying on those dozens (or thousands) of people at the bottom of the traditional pyramid. The inverted pyramid is a concept that helps me, as a leader, keep in mind that my job is to help those people do their jobs well, not just to give them directions (or, in a military context, orders) to do certain things. No, the leader's job is to communicate intention, give those people authority to do what they need to do, and deliberately develop them to do the work as it needs to be done.

*　*　*

Great leadership requires both thrust and vector. Your leadership constitution can be a great tool in helping you lead with a plan that is very detailed and is oriented around the data, the details, and the deliberateness of thinking through how you operate as a leader and how you communicate that to those around you.

The best leaders rely on a sturdy foundation in their approach to leading others to promote the whole team's success. Let's look next at three elements that help create that sturdiness.

CHAPTER 2
STURDY STOOL

Intellectual growth should commence
at birth and cease only at death.

—Albert Einstein

I often say that I have no original ideas, but I know a good idea when I see one. For example, in chapter 1, we deliberately dove into a leadership constitution concept I borrowed from Colonel Messenger. I have long made an engaged effort to learn from others and incorporate their good ideas into my leadership constitution, not just into the way I think about leadership but also into the way I lead.

The notion of a sturdy stool as a metaphor for leadership is a prime example of a great idea that I didn't originate but that I've embraced, assimilated into my leadership constitution, and tried to follow on my own leadership journey.

It's the idea of a three-legged stool that operates best, obviously, when all three legs are the same length and are properly (and evenly) affixed to the seat. Why three? This is drawn from a theory I heard about many, many years ago called the Power of Threes. The theory is that people tend to remember well things that they learn as a series, and three seems to be the magic number of elements in the series. Not that the human mind isn't capable of processing more than that, but the Power of Threes suggests there's just something about a series of three that seems to really resonate with people.

The other thing about using a three-legged stool is it's vastly superior to trying to balance on a stool with just one or two legs (enjoy that funny picture in your mind) or sitting on a rock or a floor. I like this less humorous but far more effective visual of a three-legged stool, as long as the three legs are even, equal, and firmly attached, as good framing. The legs have to be in proper balance for the stool to work well.

My own sturdy stool analogy came into its greatest focus during the last decade of my Air Force career, as I assigned each leg a specific definition. These principles and practices were things that, upon reflection, I understood much earlier in my career but hadn't labeled in the manner we will explore here. It's not that I wasn't doing these things, but reading relevant research and applying it to my leadership experience eventually crystallized my sturdy stool and helped me be much more thoughtful about what I needed to be doing as a leader.

For me, the sturdy stool has these three legs: Growth Mindset, Outward Mindset, and Psychological Safety. Each of them requires continuous and connected intellectual growth.

GROWTH MINDSET

The first leg is the idea of a growth mindset. Luckily, my entire leadership constitution doesn't have to balance on a single leg; but if it did, this would be the most important one.

The concept of growth mindset is generally attributed to an American psychologist, Dr. Carol Dweck, who began doing a great deal of research and analysis of the idea back in the late 1980s. Essentially, having a growth mindset means having intellectual curiosity and viewing ourselves as lifelong learners.

I've reframed and refined the concept over the course of my own career, and for me, maintaining a growth mindset means considering education, experience, and expertise as continuous journeys rather than destinations. As I became more senior during my Air Force career, I discovered that the need for this growth mindset actually accelerated. I never really "arrived," and I thought a lot about this. Early in our careers, a growth mindset as a continuous journey isn't truly universal to every position people pursue.

Early in our careers, the things we're required to do as leaders aren't all that expansive or extensive. The authorities we control, maybe the number of people we manage or lead, isn't very broad or deep. We can master each of those positions. But as we move upward, generally speaking, our span of control, our responsibilities, our authorities, and our time demands increase and add more and more pressure. Knowing everything about everything in our position, or mastering every single thing that we're responsible for or that we oversee, is increasingly difficult. Advance high enough, and it becomes impossible.

If we focus on crafting and curating a growth mindset, the way I think about it, we develop not just a recognition but a true understanding of personal growth as a continuous journey throughout our lives. Having thought a lot about this over time, I've often applied that great quote from Albert Einstein at the beginning of this chapter.

I love that idea. I want to stay engaged intellectually. Not that I'm "an intellectual," as in an academic sense, but I want to stay curious. I always consider that I'm still learning, still growing, still leaning into whatever I'm doing; and this applies not only to my work as a leader but wherever I'm working on the organizational chart. No matter how much time passes or how things change, I still want to be bringing value to my organization.

When I became a Brigadier (one-star) General, I worked with a four-star General named David Thompson who was, at that time, the first vice chief of Space Operations, the number two position in the US Space Force.

About six months after I pinned on my star, we were having a conversation about being a great role model—a leader who mentors people and maintains a growth mindset of their own.

General Thompson asked me how it was going. At first I thought he was simply asking how it was going in the position I held at the time: the first-ever deputy chief human capital officer for the newly formed US Space Force. But that was only part of it. He was really asking me how it was going for me as a new senior executive-level leader. How was I finding it? How was I discovering the ability to navigate this new environment, with all these new responsibilities and expectations?

Frankly, when you walk into a room carrying that rank—or when you walk in as a newly appointed chief operating officer (COO) at a company, for that matter—there are certain expectations that the men and women around us have because of the position we hold.

My reply to General Thompson was that I felt like I was starting as a brand-new second lieutenant (the most junior officer rank in the military, equivalent to an ensign in the Navy or Coast Guard). "I'm a Second Lieutenant all over again," I said. "Like I'm the Second Lieutenant of the General Officer corps. I don't know what in the world I'm really supposed to do, but people are expecting me to have answers."

He laughed. "I get that," he said. "I've been a General for ten years, and I still don't have it all figured out."

The General used a little bit of self-deprecation to communicate to me that it was okay to feel the way I did as long as I invested in continuous learning. He knew I'd learn what I needed to know, things I maybe didn't know yet, but I couldn't just rest on what had gotten me to this point and assume it would be enough to get me to the next way station.

We have to continue to be engaged in our own learning. We have to consistently maintain a growth mindset. I got a big takeaway from working with General Thompson in that I knew I was doing the right kinds of things. Though I didn't have it all in my head yet and I was never going to get to a place where I knew everything, I would get where I needed to go. That's because I had invested in this growth mindset very deliberately and had that intellectual curiosity.

I was reading, writing, researching, engaging experts on things that I didn't understand or know about, particularly about space operations (a "low-touch" area up to that point in my career). There were things I just didn't understand yet. Some were simple, like terminology for that part of the military enterprise. At first, I just needed to learn definitions to understand basic concepts to which I had not been previously exposed.

In the absence of curiosity, I suppose you could just fake it till you make it, but in an important position, that's not good enough. Not when everyone around us expects us to have answers, and we haven't yet figured out the questions.

As a young officer, I had worked for a "full-bird" colonel as her executive officer. I was basically the person who managed her schedule. I made sure that the materials she needed for every meeting were there on time and that she had the opportunity to read and review things (and do any necessary editing) in advance. Overall, it was my job just to make sure she was prepared to meet all of her responsibilities by taking some of the pressure off—not decision-making pressure, but administrative actions and other routine activities that she just didn't need to be thinking about.

My boss at that time was Colonel Peggy Shaw, one of my earliest military mentors and a truly terrific leader. One day, while we were going over papers for upcoming meetings, I remember asking her, "How do you do it?

"You go from one meeting where you're talking about financial matters to another where you're talking about logistics, to another about childcare for our men and women on the installation, to yet another where you're addressing some problem with the water quality at the base swimming pool," I said. "How do you manage all the different things you're dealing with?"

We even had a big snowstorm around that time. "For example, how do you simply jump into thinking about, and directing, snow removal with all of these other competing things for which you're responsible?" I asked.

Colonel Shaw had responsibility for all these things and much more (the first executive position I mentioned in chapter 1 that I assumed was the same position Colonel Shaw held when I worked for her). So many things she led weren't necessarily connected one to another. How did she go from one thing to the next, seemingly well read, discerning, and detailed about them, as not necessarily *the* expert but enough of an expert to make good, data-driven, deliberate decisions?

I expected her to give me an answer about having a growth mindset. About "leaning in" and reading and learning and continuously building what's in your brain. In an effort to avoid starting with some overly wonkish statement, she started with a little humor to help keep me, as a young officer, from becoming overwhelmed at the things she did to embrace and exemplify the leader she was, one of the many things I admired about her.

She said, "If you're wearing the rank, you just baffle people with BS if you can't dazzle them with brilliance. By the time they figure out you don't know what you're talking about, you've already gone on to your next assignment."

Like General Thompson when I was a new general, Colonel Shaw had the confidence to actually have a sense of humor about the topic. With a lighter mood set, we continued to talk about it, and naturally the moral of the story was that you really need to be engaged in continuous learning to juggle all the responsibilities of senior leadership. It takes time and a true growth mindset to build the capacity and capability to operate the way she and other great leaders do. (We'll discuss this particular stool leg much more in chapter 8, "Leaders Are Readers.")

OUTWARD MINDSET

That was about thirty years ago as I write these words, and I'm still remembering what Colonel Shaw said all these years later because it was funny, but it was also pointedly correct. The lesson was "Don't just try to baffle people with nonsense; actually learn and become better at your responsibilities, even if you aren't the best expert. You need to know enough to make appropriate decisions as a leader."

This led me to an exploration of the next leg of my sturdy leadership stool, the outward mindset. I understood the need to be a good teammate, and that was already part of what would become my leadership constitution. But later in my career, in 2019, I was exploring what being a good teammate meant in greater depth, especially to those of us in uniform, and that exploration led me to the work of another American psychologist from four decades earlier. In 1979, Dr. C. Terry Warner founded the Arbinger Institute, which published the book *The Outward Mindset: Seeing Beyond Ourselves*.

Just as Dr. Dweck started by saying one can either have a static mindset or a growth mindset, Dr. Warner thought about human and organizational behavior in a binary way. His work revealed an inward mindset that focuses on ourselves—our own individual and personal success or, within an organization, the success of our business unit over the success of another. I'm all for meritocracy and healthy competition, but the work of Dr. Warner, Jim Ferrell, and others at the Arbinger Institute demonstrates that when we have an outward mindset, a focus first on the success of others or of another part of the organization, we and our organization will both be much more successful.

Consider a football team. The quarterback can't win the game all by themselves. They need to have other players fulfilling their roles. And a good quarterback makes a running back or a tight end or a wide receiver better still by elevating their own play in support of others. To take this analogy further, a quarterback who's willing to make a block that allows his running back to spring from the backfield and gain eight or ten or twelve yards is demonstrating an outward mindset at that moment. He's more successful than he would be with an inward mindset that says, "I'll just hand you the ball, and you figure it out yourself," watching as the back is stopped at the line of scrimmage because no one made the block that would've opened a running lane for him.

The leader who adopts an outward mindset is always thinking, *What can I do to help my teammates be successful, perhaps even more successful than I am?*

I didn't get this right all the time. Early in my career, in particular, I got very, very focused on myself because I knew the game plan to be successful, what it would take for me to get the opportunity for promotion or the next position, so I chose to focus on that. And while I wasn't a bad teammate, my reflexive response was to think about what *I* would gain or how something would help *me*.

I wasn't trying to be a careerist for the sake of being a careerist, stepping on others to get where I wanted to go. I never did that. Rather, it was a simple inward mindset at work.

Eventually I began to think a little differently. I started to develop an appreciation for the outward mindset, even if I hadn't yet categorized it that way. I realized that if I was much more focused on making the people around me successful, then by extension, I would probably be successful, too. Even when I was leaving the team, if I'd been investing in them and trying to make them the best version of themselves, I knew the team would do better whether or not I was still leading it.

If I think of myself as the quarterback, I'll have (many) more wins in my column by approaching leadership with an outward mindset. It's like the Golden Rule, doing unto others as you'd want them to do unto you, thinking about others first. I think of the philosopher Johann Wolfgang von Goethe, who wrote that "you can easily judge the character of a man by how he treats those who can do nothing for him." I want to be a person of such character that when people get to know me, they know I'll pour myself out for a teammate even if that teammate can't help me do anything. The team will be successful even if that teammate doesn't necessarily make me individually, as the leader, successful.

That's okay because I know I've made an effort to help that other person succeed.

PSYCHOLOGICAL SAFETY

Just as Dr. Dweck defined the growth mindset, Dr. Warner and the Arbinger Institute defined the outward mindset. Exploring their work helped me put my "lifelong learner" and "good teammate" practices into frameworks that were easily understood and definable. But the stool isn't sturdy without a strong third leg. The growth mindset and outward mindset don't work without a psychologically safe environment.

There are a number of reasons this type of environment matters. These days, the "psychologically safe" label is everywhere. It's rapidly becoming an overused term and may be misunderstood as some sort of psychobabble or a touchy-feely idea. That's not what this is at all.

Let's learn from another PhD researcher, Dr. Amy C. Edmondson, a professor at Harvard Business School who's written extensively on the subject of psychological safety. When I dove deeply into this concept in her book, *The Fearless Organization: Creating Psychological Safety in the Workplace for Learning, Innovation, and Growth*, it was much more representative and reflective of my own thinking for many years. Whether or not she's the first person to ever define it, she's certainly one of the most ardent acolytes of the concept. I've heard her speak about it in person a couple of times, read a lot of her materials, and tried to put it into practice.

In my reframe, psychological safety means no one is dismissed, diminished, or demeaned for simply sharing what they're thinking. This gives the leader the opportunity to work with teammates in a very open, transparent way. As Dr. Edmondson describes it, when leaders apply psychological safety well, barriers are removed that would otherwise block things like innovation, forward movement inside an organization, or even deeper connection, collaboration, communication, and cohesion within a team. This allows for greater success because a truly safe psychological environment helps build trust in organizations and among teammates. People know they can say anything to their leader, and the leader won't come back with "Well, that's just dumb! Why would you think that?" or "That's silly" or "That won't work."

That type of reaction just shuts people down. But a leader might respond that way if they haven't deliberately created an environment of psychological safety for their team.

A good leader allows open brainstorming and conversation because they know their people's thoughts matter. In this environment, teammates realize things may not go in the direction they're recommending and their idea may not gain traction now or ever, but they're okay with that. They know they still have the opportunity to make their voice heard and what they say has value.

As leaders, we're only going to get the best out of our teams if all the team members have the opportunity to fully participate. After all, it's human nature: We all have different ways of thinking about things.

By nature, I'm more of an introvert than I am an extrovert. It's challenging for me to go into a room filled with people, even if they're people I know. It de-energizes me. I'll get a lot of energy working with a smaller group of two to four people because it's a more intimate setting and I don't feel all the stressors, the noise and distraction of having a lot of people around. As an introvert, I'd much prefer being in a room with just a couple of people rather than a thousand people. It's not because I dislike people but because I know what will give me energy as opposed to taking energy from me. Psychological safety is another way for me to be considerate of others and their needs.

For some people, particularly extroverts, big rooms are no problem. They'll tell us what they're thinking, and they're fully engaged and fully present. But when we have introverts in the room, or people of any type who are more reserved, how do we draw them into the conversation? Psychological safety is about making sure everybody has value and voice inside the organization and deliberately creating conditions that let them speak up.

John C. Maxwell is one of my favorite leadership exemplars, famous for all kinds of great quotes and ideas. One that I've used over the years is this: "People don't care how much you know until they know how much you care."

When leaders apply this thinking, starting from the perch and perspective of caring enough to hear what people have to say, it creates opportunities and openings for them to share their thinking without being judged good, bad, or indifferent for it. Psychological safety means being deliberate about making sure teammates have that opportunity.

A leader's deliberate effort to create an environment of true psychological safety goes a long way when it's tied to the other legs of the stool. When we commit to continually learn and grow personally, to constantly focus on making our teammates successful, and to give others the opportunity to be fully heard, there's almost nothing our organizations can't do.

In a psychologically safe environment, it's not only okay to speak up but to challenge. Everyone has the opportunity to provide counter-discussion to any point. As leaders, we might offer our thinking on a matter, and of course there will be times when we can't overthink or try to over-communicate. A decision needs to be made. A leader is ultimately responsible for making the best decision possible based on the information available at the time. More often than not, a decision doesn't need to be made immediately. We have time to think about it, seek advice and counsel, and get some counterpoints or counterfactuals. And in a psychologically safe environment, we can more easily do that. Without it, someone who might have a better approach to solving a problem, launching a new product, or serving a key customer might not be heard, and a big opportunity could be lost.

We're only going to get the best and brightest ideas in an environment where people know they can voice their thoughts without being diminished or demeaned.

I've seen things go badly for this very reason. In one of the organizations I led toward the end of my Air Force career, we put these three legs of the stool into a document called "How We Work." This was a framework for the way we operated. The document included "Here's how you hold me accountable as the leader," "Here's how you hold one another accountable," "Here's how we gain transparency in this organization," and, most importantly, "Here's how we develop trust in one another inside this organization."

For many, many years I've said that organizations operate at the speed of trust. In the absence of trust, they can't perform at their very best. When we laid out the concept of psychological safety in the last position I held in the Air Force before my retirement, a couple of teammates didn't get this quite right. They weren't mal-intended, they just misunderstood. When I said, "Psychological safety gives you the opportunity to say what's on your mind," I didn't properly put parameters on that. I wasn't trying to stifle speech, but I didn't mean that being angry, upset, or frustrated with somebody gave a person permission to say things that are caustic. In an environment of true psychological safety, we still have to be thoughtful about what we're saying and how we're saying it.

We had a couple of teammates who were openly deriding another teammate. They thought they were being constructively critical and trying to help that person rethink or think differently about a particular subject. But when I read the messages they sent, I realized they weren't understanding that psychological safety is not saying anything they wanted to say in any manner they wanted to say it. We still have to be professional in content and communication. We can provide constructive criticism, but we don't have the right to be obtuse or obnoxious.

Once we were able to reframe the concept a little bit, people understood. They realized they needed to be more thoughtful about the exact words they used, though they still had a right to offer feedback.

During my time in the Air Force, in our professional military education, we often looked at case studies of leaders who failed and what typically led to the failures. One example was the explosion of the space shuttle *Challenger* in 1986, a case we've talked about for decades. There were statisticians and scientists who knew the tolerances of the O-rings that failed, ultimately leading to the explosion of the boosters and the catastrophic destruction and loss of life. The leadership lesson is great because there were people who knew about the risk but didn't feel they had the opportunity to voice their concerns to the right people. The term *psychological safety* may have come later, but it was the absence of such an environment that led to the catastrophe. NASA is known as a no-fail organization and was the gold standard of safety and good practice. Yet what many would regard as a little thing—the lack of the right environment for discussion and dissent—led to a much bigger disaster. It might be an oversimplification, but had NASA been a psychologically safe environment where people could raise red flags with comfort, knowing their voices wouldn't be quashed by "No, no, we've already delayed the launch a couple of times, we have to get this launch up. Our window is closing and we have things we need to accomplish," that disaster might have been avoided.

In a military context, life and death decisions do have to be made, but most decisions are not life or death. It isn't just acceptable but *necessary* to open up the dialogue and create an environment in which people know they can communicate, be involved, be immersed, and share what they're thinking. And they need to know it will be heard by leaders throughout the organization.

Every opinion doesn't have to be accepted, and a psychologically safe environment doesn't have to change many or most decisions. When a leader invites different opinions but those contributions never change the leader's trajectory or decision, I would argue that leader isn't terribly open. They're going through the motions. If we're seeking more input, we're going to make better decisions, and our decisions will be shaped differently.

As a leader, many times when I thought about making a decision, I didn't have it right. As an example, as I shared earlier, the squadron commander occupies the most important leadership position in the Air Force. When I went to a similar position two years after the colleague we highlighted did, I had a specific program in mind. I believed it would provide great service and support for morale, welfare, and recreation programs that we deliver to our military members, their families, and retirees.

"This is going to be a great program," I said. My accountant replied, "Well, I don't see it in the projection. I hear what you're saying, but I don't think this is going to work here." And even though I'd given him the opportunity to share that information with me, I had already decided we were going ahead with the program. We invested five thousand dollars into it, and my accountant turned out to be right. It failed.

This taught me a valuable lesson not quite halfway through my military career. It's not good enough to let people add their opinions to the recipe if we, as leaders, have already pre-baked the decision. In that case, I had already decided that I was right and the accountant was incorrect in his analysis. Here, the outcome wasn't just a recognition that I was wrong. I went back to him and told him that I should have paid more attention to his good analysis and advice. We would've saved those dollars. What's more, as I've done at other times when I made mistakes, I didn't have this conversation with the accountant alone in his office. I told the entire leadership team that he had been right and I had gotten it wrong.

"I'm going to be better at listening to what you're saying to me," I told him, "and at making better-informed decisions based on input. I won't assume that because I've seen something work elsewhere successfully, it's going to work here."

For a good leader, having a psychologically safe environment means not only that teammates are allowed to say things but that we ourselves are allowed to change direction or modify a decision based on the input we receive.

* * *

That's a sturdy stool on which to rest our leadership constitution. A deliberate effort to keep a growth mindset, an outward mindset, and an environment of true psychological safety makes for a powerful leadership combination.

A great leader truly values all three legs of the sturdy stool. And a great leader knows that sticking to the right values is essential for success, both for the leader and for the organization as a whole.

CHAPTER 3
VALUE VALLEYS
VS. PEAK PERFORMANCE

Character, in the long run, is the decisive factor in the
life of an individual and of nations alike.

—Teddy Roosevelt

Before we built the US Space Force, late in my Air Force career, I was assigned a senior leadership and command role at the United States Air Force Academy in Colorado. At the Academy, there's a building called Polaris Hall, and that name reminds me of an important feature of great leadership: a solid understanding of "true north."

We often refer to it as the North Star, as I mentioned in the introduction, but its astronomical name is Polaris. Perhaps Polaris Hall is named after that star to remind cadets and commanders alike that a great leader always has a sense of their true north—the core set of personal values that forms the basis of their conduct and behavior.

"True North" isn't the whole of our character, but it's a big, important part. It goes beyond having a sense of right and wrong, or understanding the difference between ethical and unethical behavior, or even the difference between what's legal and what's illegal. Those are important things to grasp, no matter what profession we choose to pursue. But when it comes to our true north, we have to start with something bigger.

What do we really believe in? What do we value? If we think about things like hard work, being a good student, and learning along the way as we discussed in the last chapter, we start to form the underpinnings of character—things that are important to us and that we commit to continually work on.

I think about leadership very much like a garden we have to continually tend. If we plant the seeds but don't water the garden, provide nutrients, and pull out weeds when they come up, or if we fail to place the garden where it will get sufficient direct sunlight, then it's not going to grow. In the same way, leading starts with planting those true north seeds—core values.

I think of these seeds in terms of personal true north and professional true north, and the personal certainly impacts the professional. When we're committed to operating from our personal true north, we really can't separate who we are at work from who we are at home for very long before people will see it's a facade. If we don't have a good basis for how we choose to lead, and there's a disconnect between our personal and professional behavior, it will show. People will eventually see through it.

One example: If we're dishonest with our spouse, our children, or anyone in our immediate sphere of influence, we're also going to be dishonest at work. Probably more so, because in some respects there's less accountability at work than at home.

We have to make sure we're congruent in our personal and professional lives. If we value truth, beauty, goodness, and things that are edifying, we're likely to export that from our personal life into our professional life. That's not to say we have to reveal at work every detail about who we are personally. There is such a thing as being overly emotive or overly engaged. But again, that foundation really matters. If we're going to be successful as leaders, then that congruence will come out and people will see us as trustworthy, as someone who is tested and tempered, as reliable not just in good operating times but also in the difficult and challenging times that every organization goes through.

We each have to create our own true north, stay focused on it, and revisit it regularly. As in the analogy of the garden, we have to tend it. We can't just plant it, walk away, and trust that it's going to be great for the duration of our professional lives.

PILLARS OF RESILIENCE

Part of the personal piece of this is a leader's resilience, something we value highly in the military context. We think about resilience in four different ways, which we call "resiliency pillars": social, spiritual, mental, and physical. Similar to the sturdy stool, with three legs working in concert, these four pillars form this foundational value.

Take social resilience, for example. If you're introverted like me, to be successful in a professional setting, you can still be introverted, but you have to be able to work in a way that seems extroverted. At times, I've found myself in settings with hundreds or even thousands of people, which really draws energy out of me (whereas a true extrovert would become more energized by such a situation). I learned throughout my career that I needed to develop the social resilience to connect with the people in my close circle in a good way.

Spiritual resilience doesn't necessarily mean being religious, but as a person of faith, this matters to me deeply, so I work at tending that part of my garden routinely—not just every Sunday but throughout the week.

And when we think about building and maintaining physical resilience, it's as simple as exercising, whatever that looks like for each leader. Maybe you like to run, bike, lift weights, or hike, but whatever your preferred activity, that physical action is good for you. We know that physiologically and psychologically, there's a release of good hormones in the body when we exercise.

Mental resilience, for me, takes a couple of different forms. I'm an intellectually curious person, so I spend a lot of time reading, and we'll discuss that more a little later in the book. I need that stimulation to keep my mind engaged, to keep me thinking, to keep me mentally focused and sharp. But I also recognize when I need to take a pause from all the noise of the day. For example, everything the brain consumes, whether it's a text, an email, a chat, a phone call, or a conversation, works the brain. The brain is working all the time. There are periods when I just need some quietness. That doesn't mean anything as extreme as being in a hyperbaric chamber, but I need some form of quiet escape to maintain my mental resilience over time.

PEAK PERFORMANCE

Focusing on these pillars of resilience helps maintain a clear core character and ensures a consistent sense of self-value. That value isn't just about what's ethical, moral, and legal; it's also the value of taking care of yourself by maintaining all the pillars. If we don't, we won't perform at peak, at least not for very long. If we're not tending the garden, so to speak, we're not cultivating the things that lend themselves to high performance, let alone peak performance.

We started the process of building the Space Force at the Pentagon just a couple of months before the start of the COVID-19 pandemic. When the pandemic struck, just as organizations worldwide did, we started closing things down. We were basically forced out of the Pentagon because we had to adhere to "social distancing." There was concern at the Pentagon that having 25,000 people together every single day may not have been a great way to slow the spread of the disease. So we went from that high number in the building to about 5,000. That's an 80 percent reduction, and after the first few weeks of the shutdown, I sometimes found myself working alone in a space where there might normally be a hundred or more people. It was kind of dystopian. If there had been wild animals running the corridors and plant overgrowth all over the place, like in futuristic dystopian or post-apocalyptic movies, it probably would have felt much more appropriate.

However, the building was purified and pristine. It was still being cleaned regularly, but those of us working in the building during those days often didn't see another human for hours on end. That social connection, mental stimulation, and physical support we get by being in a room with somebody else and having interpersonal human contact was basically taken away. I couldn't go to my fitness center, I couldn't go to my church at the time, and I was living apart from my family (they were 180 miles from the office). There were long stretches of, frankly, loneliness and too much quiet. All the things that were normally available to help me tend to those resiliency pillars and maintain self-value were not accessible or available.

By August 2020, roughly six months into the pandemic, I was in a very bad place. Back then, many people talked about "the COVID ten" (or sometimes fifteen), which was a real thing because it was very easy to put on an extra ten or fifteen pounds during that shutdown. In many cases, we were working from home, and it was too easy to just go to the kitchen twenty feet away and snack all day. On top of that, we weren't exercising.

I wasn't sleeping well, I was having nightmares, and it took my wife understanding and being sensitive to the fact that something was not good with me to pull me out of it. She was able to help me recenter and recognize the things I should have been doing that I wasn't. The fitness centers were closed, but that didn't stop me from going outside for a run or a walk, or from doing calisthenics or basic exercises with home equipment. I could have done that much. I mean, we can do a push-up or sit-up anywhere. We don't need equipment to do that. I was also making choices with my diet that weren't good for me. In general, I wasn't taking care of my physical resilience pillar. I finally realized it was time to make different choices and get back to my more helpful and healthy physical routine, including both exercise and diet.

At this point, I still couldn't go to church, but there were podcasts available, and eventually my congregation figured out how to get together using a video-conferencing application. I became mindful that there are alternative ways to take care of that spiritual resilience pillar, too. After all, my Bible and shelves full of books were available to me.

For mental resilience, there were plenty of things I could do that didn't require some of the facilities where I might usually go to stimulate my mind. Just because the libraries weren't easily accessible or convenient didn't mean I couldn't get online, buy books, or work through other resources.

It's all connected.

Once I got back to tending my resilience pillars and got my self-value back in shape, that allowed me to make sure my performance returned to a high level, particularly during this very difficult time. I was helping to build the first new military service in more than seventy years in the middle of a global pandemic while being geographically separated from my family. To return to high performance, I had to refocus on the things that mattered so that they would continue to undergird who I was both personally and professionally. Operating from a firm foundation of those values was crucial to restoring and returning me to peak performance.

VALUE VALLEYS: VALUING THE WRONG THINGS

Throughout my military career, we talked about this notion that as long as a proposed decision or action wasn't unethical, immoral, or illegal, the answer was "Yes! What was the question?"

Eventually we talked about these things in different terms: "It's a *qualified* yes. We just need to figure out how we can get to where we want to go."

If we value the wrong things—for instance, if someone values success at any expense—then we're likely to fail. If there's a gap, or a lapse, in what we think is ethical behavior, we're going to fail. We might be successful for years, even decades, but eventually we're going to fail. And this really gets to the idea that we must have good, if not great, character, because it will impact our performance.

Early in my Air Force career, I figured out that there was a kind of road map to success. It was ideal to be Professional of the Quarter or Professional of the Year and to get the "hardware" (trophies, plaques, or other tokens of recognition). When we went to various training and development programs, we wanted to be the distinguished graduate or the top graduate or have the highest grade point average. All those things would accrue to our benefit.

The way we look at those things in our annual performance reviews, like many companies do, is that if we've started to pull a number of those things together, we've created a positive snowball effect in our careers in which a couple little things gradually accumulate into bigger things, or success.

Those bits of hardware are sometimes little more than proxy indicators. I may have been the best professional over that quarter, but that doesn't mean I was the best over a longer time horizon or that I consistently maintained peak performance.

In trying to follow this road map, my focus shifted toward putting myself in for every opportunity to win an award, to get recognition, to be the person on the stage or in the spotlight. I did not get to the point of stepping on others to get there or using unethical means, but my focus was wrong. I was focused on winning awards rather than achieving the highest possible performance.

Eventually, as my wife challenged me on that inward focus, I came to question this drive for recognition:

- I did great, but was I focused on the team or organizational outcomes first?
- Was I truly performing well? Was this my very best?
- Was I the kind of person and professional that people wanted to follow? I was honing my leadership skills, but were people looking at me and thinking, *Whatever he's doing is really working; we're a high-performing team, and I would follow that human anywhere,* or did they have the impression that I was only chasing the recognition?

If my individual performance was really good, that's okay, but it shouldn't have been my primary focus. It's possible to be the star on a failing team when you aren't focused on the team more than on yourself.

In addition to my wife holding me accountable to a higher conduct standard, I had a supervisor who gave me a seven-page feedback document at this point in my career. Even now, decades later, no one has given me anything quite that lengthy. She also helped me see that I was too focused on the spotlight and not focused enough on being a true peak performer, not in it for myself but in it as a team member working to make others successful.

This goes back to the outward mindset in the prior chapter. I needed to be even more focused on others. While I had wanted to help my teams be effective and accomplish our goals and objectives, in the back of my mind I was thinking, *Okay, we're going to do that, and then I'm going to find a way to use our success to my benefit.*

That feedback session was added confirmation that I was in a "value valley." The feedback was good for me because it helped me recognize that my highest value at that time was the wrong one. It showed me that, over time, if I didn't change my focus, I could become a toxic leader as opposed to being a good leader who focused on the team's success first and foremost. It gave me the opportunity to course-correct early in my career, and I'm very grateful for it.

At the time, I was very upset about that feedback because it felt like a personal attack. I needed to step away from it. It actually took me a few months to get through all of that, mentally. But after some real reflection, I recognized that the leader who took the time to deliver that feedback did me a great service in helping me see what I wasn't seeing in myself.

Over time, I was able to be more reflective about it and respond in an appropriate manner. Not just to react but to actually respond, meaning to make smart decisions about that feedback to become a better performer and to get to peak performance through energizing and engaging the right values. The interventions from both my wife and my boss at that time, early enough in my career, allowed me to start to see the same thing in others.

There came a number of times in my career when I saw that people were in the same value valley. In some cases they were focused, like I had been, on just being in the spotlight as opposed to being the person that everybody goes to because they seem to have everything working really well. For example, I had a teammate at the Air Force Academy who I recognized had fallen into this value valley. To this day, I believe this particular professional is one of the top five best I've known throughout my Air Force career at the particular specialty in which they were working. What happened, though, was that while this person was a peak performer on the outside, they fell into a value valley inside and became toxic. They were leading by fear and intimidation as opposed to leading with better characteristics that would inspire people to perform, work hard, and do their best. It should have been the focus to create an environment in which the team knew this person valued them, heard them, shared their vision with them, and could be trusted. And because they hadn't had the interventions I'd had earlier in my career, this leader had created an environment that was really bad for the Academy.

I removed that person from a position of leadership. It wasn't a hard decision to make. But it's still hard to do when you care about someone as a human being, a person, and a professional. It was essential, though, to help that person see that they had entered a value valley and how that had negatively affected their performance and that of the team they were charged with leading. They were valuing the wrong things, and by recognizing it, I helped them avoid remaining in the value valley before irreparable harm might have taken hold

Returning to the garden example, we have to pull the weeds out for the whole garden to be healthy. So as difficult as it was to remove this person from leadership, I knew it was the right thing to do for the organization. If we were going to reach peak performance, it had to be done. It seemed clear that a performance improvement plan was not going to help this person, particularly when they were in more senior leadership, and the likelihood that we could groom or grow them to peak performance in that position was not high.

Leadership requires making the hard calls, pulling ourselves out of our own value valleys, recognizing the value valleys of the people around us, and responding thoughtfully and thoroughly in those situations. And it's about managing our resilience and keeping what we in the military refer to as the "human weapon system" fully intact, fully engaged, and ready for the work. If we can collectively stay out of the value valleys, then we're going to perform much better as a team.

* * *

The bottom line: To reach peak performance, we have to stay out of the value valleys. One way my wife encouraged me to think about this is to apply what is written in the Bible in Philippians 2:3 (ESV): *"Do nothing from selfish ambition or conceit, but in humility count others more significant than yourselves. Let each of you look not only to his own interests, but also to the interests of others."* Living and leading this way helps maintain humility and a focus on vital values.

Speaking of peaks and valleys, the geographic setting of the US Air Force Academy, nestled in the foothills of the majestic Rocky Mountains, is inspiring. Our future leaders learn and train in an environment full of peaks and valleys. To use that setting as a metaphor, it's really important to recognize that we're not automatons, we're not robots, and we're not machines. We're human beings. We all face times when we seem to be walking through valleys created when we slip into focusing on the wrong things. This is where having really good teammates and building good leadership skills helps us recognize when teammates are headed into a valley. A great leader can try to make the value valley less steep or help a teammate who is already in the valley successfully navigate back out of it, giving them a chance to climb back to their peak personal and professional performance.

Mountain climbers know that, at times, they'll climb to the top of a mountain only to discover that they've reached a false summit. Only then can they see that, to reach the true peak, they have more climbing to do. Reaching that summit was an accomplishment, but they haven't really peaked yet. Undeterred, the best climbers take a deep breath and look for the path that will take them all the way to the top. Let's look next at how the best leaders do the very same thing.

PART II
LEADING FOR VICTORY

Talent hits a target no one else can hit.
Genius hits a target no one else can see.
—Arthur Schopenhauer

CHAPTER 4
BIG, BOLD, BEYOND

Every day, you may make progress.
Every step may be fruitful.
Yet there will stretch out before you an ever-
lengthening, ever-ascending, ever-improving path.
You know you will never get to the end of the journey.
But this, so far from discouraging, only adds to the joy
and glory of the climb.

—Sir Winston Churchill

"Big, bold, and beyond," besides being a nice alliteration, is about having true leadership vision and about where that can take an organization.

Assuming we've stayed out of the value valley, or that we've come out of the value valley and we're moving back toward peak performance (for ourselves and our team), we have a vision. We have an idea of where we want to take the organization. Most leaders and organizations I've been around do have a mission statement, a vision statement, and objectives, but far too often, coming up with these declarations becomes an exercise in merely checking a box. Of course, we have to have an organizational mission and vision statement, but those are often two-dimensional, static, or inactive documents or statements.

Great leadership is about understanding where we're going and continuing to act and lead activities that are going to reach and realize the vision. The mission is what we do. It's the good, the service, the product that we deliver to a customer. Or, in a military context, if we're supposed to be launching aircraft, it's doing what it takes to launch the right number for each day's mission requirements. Figuring these things out for ourselves and for our organization is a central component of what good leaders do.

Strengthening our personal resilience is a good place to start. As leaders, it's on us to know the vision—not just for the organizations we lead but for ourselves. What are we trying to accomplish, personally, as leaders? What's our vision? What would we like to accomplish in our own lives, and how is that mutually supportive or supported by what we do professionally?

I often share that the reason I stayed in the Air Force for thirty years is that I loved the work we as a team and an organization were accomplishing, and understanding that was my mission. That was based on having a shared vision.

We understood where we were going. Every leader I've worked with or for, including these days in the private sector, has had a vision of where we're going as an organization.

The best leaders also understand that we have to be willing to flex in a different direction when necessary. There are likely thousands of great business case studies to show what happens when we lose the ability to be alert, agile, and adaptive. We can't simply set a vision once and assume it won't shift later as we come into contact with actual market conditions.

Blockbuster Video is a great example of this. Most people who are around my age, pretty close to it, or older, remember the days when we used to go to a video store to rent VHS tapes (or, later, DVDs) when it was time for movie night at home. Blockbuster was one of the biggest, if not the biggest, chain of such stores. It was an activity we looked forward to on Friday or Saturday night: We'd go to Blockbuster, rent a couple of movies, and then pick up a pizza or other favorite "fat" food on the way home or make popcorn in the microwave.

Blockbuster grew to the point where it not only had the largest market share in the video rental space but the market capital to invest in the next step, such as launching a digital platform. Its leaders could have created a mail-rental business in the interim.

That's how Netflix got its start.

Today, Netflix is streaming all on-demand content. But their first, original business model was to mail the DVDs that customers ordered online. Typically the disk arrived in a couple of days, and we could watch it as many times as we wanted. We didn't have to rewind DVDs like we did the VHS tapes from Blockbuster to avoid a rewind fee. Then, when the rental period was over, we simply dropped the disk back in the mailer and sent it back to Netflix.

You might not know that Netflix presented that idea to Blockbuster, and Blockbuster decided brick-and-mortar stores were the way to go. Its decision-makers walked away from the model Netflix presented. Yes, Blockbuster had the opportunity in the early days to listen to this idea but decided to stick with its "proven" business model instead.

Netflix's vision is really important here. All along, its leaders believed the company would eventually get to an on-demand streaming capability. The mail-order model was just a stepping stone to the digital service. Netflix's vision wasn't really mail-order movies; it was on-demand streaming services. And as you probably know, in time, the company started to develop its own content, like a Hollywood studio. The long-term Netflix vision is about continuing to advance in an internet-based entertainment business.

This example demonstrates a kind of continuum for a vision, looking beyond the current market conditions and way into the future.

Another example is Apple. When Steve Jobs came up with the iPod, he didn't intend to stop there. The iPhone was what he was actually working toward. But the technology needed time to catch up with his vision. So, Jobs launched the iPod, then eventually added iTunes so we could download music digitally (and avoid having to buy CDs). Now we could stream music, and later podcasts, on our cool new iPods.

But the vision was still to get to the iPhone. It wasn't about just being able to download music or podcasts. And of course, now on any smart device, you can download everything—all kinds of digital media, music, movies, books, and on and on. Oh, and it's also a camera. And a telephone. And a computer, right there in your pocket or purse. That was what Jobs and Apple were always trying to get to, and they realized the iPod was only a step toward that greater technological marvel.

A vision motivates us to constantly reach for the next thing. It's not about just looking into the future and dreaming. It's thinking backward: *This is where I really want us to go as an organization and where I want to go as a leader.* It's about figuring out what steps we can take now, tracing backward from that bigger vision in the future.

This means we have to set goals as leaders, we have to share them, and we have to be willing to adjust them over time. Great leaders do this by setting and communicating objectives called SMART goals:

- Specific
- Measurable
- Achievable
- Relevant
- Time-bound

SMART GOALS

In 1981, a professor and consultant named George T. Doran published an article entitled "There's a S.M.A.R.T. Way to Write Management's Goals and Objectives." While the concept has since been refined by various thinkers, the basic framework has stood the test of time and is still used throughout countless organizations. Using Doran's framework, leaders create goals with five key elements.

Specific. Rather than stating a goal to "become healthier," for example, a SMART goal would include specific health objectives, such as losing weight, exercising more, and sticking to a sensible diet.

Measurable. It's important to create goals related to measurable activities so everyone can see when/if the team is making progress toward its overall objective. Using the health example above, an individual might set measurable goals such as "lose ten pounds," "work out for thirty minutes, four days per week," or "limit calorie intake to 2,000 daily."

Achievable. Sometimes we set grand goals that are not achievable in a way that can be communicated to the team in the here and now. Instead of setting goals that might be achievable in the future, we have to focus on what's achievable in the near to midterm to realize the broader future vision.

Relevant. Today's goals have to be achievable today and have to relate to the broader long-term vision as present-day steps toward future success. Steve Jobs probably established many achievable short-term goals leading to the introduction of the iPod but knew that product would represent only a step toward the grander vision of the iPhone.

Time-bound. Finally, the leader has to establish a deadline for the achievement of each objective, which facilitates movement to the next phase in a timely fashion (for instance, in time to meet market demands).

As leaders, if we have a great vision but we don't have goals that are specific and achievable, regularly measured, relevant and realistic, time-bound, and supportive of our organization's desired trajectory, our goals won't be as effective as they could be.

MOON SHOTS

It's okay to take moon shots. In fact, a leader with great vision almost always does.

The idea of the moon shot is widely attributed to President John F. Kennedy, who declared in the early 1960s—years before anyone thought it possible—that the United States would put a man on the moon by the end of that decade.

I wasn't alive at the time, but my reading of historical documents indicates that many people thought Kennedy's idea was nuts. Indeed, at that point we were very early in the space race against the Soviet Union. We had limited capabilities. We were doing some things with more advanced propulsion and rocketry, and we had some successful orbital launches and that sort of thing, but traveling to the moon seemed out of reach. That's why grand visions, like the one Jobs had for the iPhone, are often called "moon shots."

A moon shot is a stretch goal. Kennedy believed that over time, taking the right steps and knocking down achievable goals, we could eventually put a man on the moon. As it turned out, by the end of the decade (in July 1969), we did exactly that.

A good leader sets stretch targets and takes moon shots. We shouldn't aim to get over such low bars that we can successfully navigate every single one every single time. We have to stretch ourselves. We also have to make sure that we have good feedback loops and that we adjust our goals for the right reasons, not just because we're looking for ways to appear successful.

As an example, at the Air Force Academy, we monitored a number of monthly, quarterly, semi-annual, and annual metrics. One of those was the in-service rate of our vehicles. At the time, our government fleet had 330 vehicles. It had the largest number of buses in the entire Air Force, which makes sense because the Air Force Academy is a college as well as a military installation—freshman and sophomore cadets aren't permitted to bring their personal vehicles to the Academy, so we needed buses to transport them to events, such as academic and athletic competitions. My chief logistician would proudly share, month after month, that the in-service vehicle rate usually came in at 97.5 percent. The Air Force target was 94 percent or higher.

For many months and quarters in a row, we exceeded (and usually well exceeded) the Air Force standard. After some time, I asked, "Why don't we stretch that upward?

Why simply pat ourselves on the back? Why not make our own standard 98 percent and try to work a little harder?" There would be a positive mission impact if we improved our in-service vehicle rate, and that's if 98 percent was actually achievable.

It wasn't about just letting ourselves off the hook. It was about stretching to achieve more. One of the ways I asked the team to be thoughtful about that in-service measurement was to say, "We're always hitting 97.5 percent, always in the green, and always doing well. But what's in the 2.5 percent that are not in service?"

The chief logistician wasn't sure during that particular meeting. My point was that we needed to know about those out-of-service vehicles because that's where the real danger lurks. Something in that 2.5 percent could have an outsized impact on our ability to achieve our mission or greater goals.

We had five woodland firefighting vehicles in our firefighting inventory. Just five. The Air Force Academy is 17,455 acres or 30.5 square miles of land, the size of many cities. It's a pretty large area. And 70–75 percent of that area was still woodland. It was undeveloped. In and around Colorado Springs, as in other regions, particularly in the Southwest and toward the West Coast, dry conditions prevail. As a result, the likelihood of a fire is often elevated. As far as I was concerned, as the person responsible for that area, including (at the time) 343 academic and other work buildings, 632 homes, 172 miles of paved roads, 73 miles of unpaved roads, and tens of thousands of trees, it wasn't a matter of whether there would be a woodland fire; it was a question of when. Would we be prepared?

We did have a small fire when I was in my key senior leadership position there, and thankfully it was contained very quickly. But my point was this: If two of our five woodland firefighting vehicles were out of service, only 60 percent of our capacity would be available to fight any fire when it erupted, even though the installation was still at a 97.5 percent vehicle in-service rate—well above the Air Force goal but possibly well below the practical needs of that installation in that one mission-critical area. I wouldn't have been as concerned if I had a number of buses out of commission, because I could always go into town and contract more buses if needed. But I couldn't, in the emergency situation of a fire, go downtown and find additional woodland firefighting vehicles available.

It was about challenging the team to look in the red portion of the metrics so that we could reduce, if not eliminate, risk. We could set a higher stretch goal and become even better still at what we were doing. I was trying to shift the team's vision from just celebrating that we continually met or exceeded the metric to recognizing an opportunity to think differently. Let's stretch ourselves and have a broader vision.

LOON SHOTS

Once we've stretched to reach some of these higher goals— once we've taken some moon shots—why not take a couple of "loon shots"?

A loon shot is beyond the moon shot. The concept comes from a 2019 book by physicist and technologist Safi Bahcall entitled *Loonshots: How to Nurture the Crazy Ideas That Win Wars, Cure Diseases, and Transform Industries.* In this book, Bahcall advances the notion of setting a course to achieve things that people think are impossible. It means recognizing that you're not going to get there overnight but truly contemplating how you can stretch your mind "past going to the moon."

As of this writing, Elon Musk is planning to put a human on Mars. That's a loon shot. It's so far beyond what we've been able to do so far, even having gone to the moon. How do we accomplish this crazy goal?

When Steve Jobs first tried to get to the iPhone, that was in fact a loon shot, as Safi Bahcall shares in his book.

You might guess that the term *loon shot* comes from the word *lunacy* or *lunatic*, and Bahcall does suggest these are crazy ideas. But a loon shot is such an audacious goal, it's hard for people to get their minds around it. That said, I still believe now what I believed when I read the book many years ago: As leaders, we have to have at least one loon shot goal, something we would never have imagined ourselves or our organizations doing.

For me, writing this book is a bit of a loon shot. I don't consider myself an author in that sense. It's not a particularly comfortable thing for me to do. It's not easy, and it's a really big, audacious goal for me. Now, this isn't like curing cancer, creating the iPhone, or developing a rocket that can be recovered on land and reused. But for me, it's a loon shot.

What's a loon shot for you?

That's a question I posed to most of my teammates, particularly during the last few years before I retired from the Air Force. What's your loon shot? What's that one thing, personal or professional, that you would aim for if you had all the necessary resources, all the time, all the drive, dedication, and devotion to achieve it? What would be your crazy, audacious accomplishment?

I laugh a little when thinking back on this question because many people shared the same loon shot I'm undertaking. Others shared things like "I'd love to climb Mount Everest." For others, it was as simple as "I'm not a runner, but one day I would love to run the Boston Marathon." For these people, those are big, bold, and beyond stretch goals.

Those are personal goals. Other people mentioned professional loon shots. As a young prior enlisted person who found his way to becoming a general officer, I accomplished something that would have seemed like a loon shot when I was a young professional. I would have looked at anyone who suggested I could become a general officer and said, "That's lunacy! There's no way that's ever going to happen for me."

However, it did. And it was, in part, about setting that bar higher and higher as my career progressed.

As leaders, it's not just about having vision and setting good objectives and measurable goals that we revisit over time. We also have to inspire others to go after their own personal and professional goals and give them the confidence that they can actually do it. It's important to continue to challenge them and to develop them appropriately to reach higher and higher for other objectives and outcomes they might not otherwise see for themselves. I believe a leader is responsible for developing other leaders, and some of the ways we do that are by setting a vision, making it clear, creating goals and objectives, assigning some moon shots so we can knock down big targets and accomplish big things along the way, and aiming for at least one big loon shot—something so far out there, it might seem impossible but isn't. It's just going to take more time, effort, energy, and expertise to get there.

We have to believe we can actually do it. Some of the best leaders I ever worked for (including General Darren McDew, about whom we'll talk more in the next chapter) set some of those stretch targets for me and helped me believe I could do just about anything I wanted to in the Air Force if I just believed in myself. They inspired me to set my own vision high enough that I could see past the imaginary hurdle of what was right in front of me, and to see what was possible by having vision that was outward and upward looking (not just downward and inside my current set of circumstances). How could I see that future and realize myself in it?

* * *

One of my children's high school friends, a teenager at the time, used to say, "You just have to visualize your success." It may sound simplistic, but it's astounding to me because I knew that at sixteen or seventeen years old, that young man believed in what he was saying. It resonated with me. He's right. You have to be able to visualize your own success, and that starts with having a vision that's outward and upward looking. As Churchill's words wisely imparted at the beginning of this chapter, every day, you may make progress. Every step may be fruitful.

Yet there will stretch out before you an ever-lengthening, ever-ascending, ever-improving path.

It takes more than thinking big, bold, and beyond and having the competence to pursue our vision; it takes considerable and calculated courage. Let's look at that key leadership element next.

CHAPTER 5
HAVE COURAGE, LEAD BOLDLY

If you want to make everyone happy,
don't be a leader. Sell ice cream.

—Steve Jobs

In 2016, I had the opportunity to work for one of my leadership heroes, General Darren McDew. At that time, he was the commander of the United States Transportation Command, a four-star general, and one of the most senior military leaders in the Department of Defense. I had read an article that quoted him from a few years earlier, when he was commanding the Eighteenth Air Force as a three-star general. Asked about his leadership philosophy, he had summed it up in four words: "Have courage, lead boldly."

When I read that article, I was headed to Scott Air Force Base near St. Louis, home to Eighteenth Air Force, to take over command of the base's Mission Support Group (think of that role as the "city manager" for the installation). General McDew was in my direct chain of command, albeit several levels above me, and his words from that article really resonated with me. I believed in what he was getting at, and I framed it this way: Leaders need to outthink, outpace, and outmaneuver their potential adversaries (or competitors in a private-sector context).

I was thinking about those words from a public sector (military) standpoint, but of course there are private sector applications of General McDew's leadership philosophy. It applies to any type of organization—business, for-profit, nonprofit, or public sector—because it's about a mindset. It's about thinking bigger, beyond what we might think about inside our respective roles and responsibilities. "Have courage, lead boldly" really began to put forth for me this idea that to be successful (in my case, as a new senior leader in the Air Force), a leader had to have courage of their convictions, of their experience, of their expertise, and of their education to date. And they had to point those convictions toward taking bold action while sitting on that sturdy stool we discussed in chapter 2.

As I entered my first "O-6" or "full-bird colonel" command, I adopted these four words as my tagline. It was my way of recognizing that leaders don't have all the answers, though at times those around us (subordinates, peers, or superiors) expect us to. And, as we also covered in my earlier email tagline example, here, I set about making sure my entire 1,520-person team knew exactly what I meant by those four words. It wasn't a simple statement or bumper sticker; rather, it informed and influenced the vision we set and pursued together.

I knew I didn't have all the answers. Even now, as a former C-suite executive, I still don't. In my new civilian sector career, I work with C-suite executive clients, and I had to have confidence and courage to step into that role following my Air Force retirement.

As a longtime military member, I know courage is not just about combat or physical action (taking that hill, flying that aircraft into a terribly dangerous zone, or any other act of military bravery). It's important for a leader to look at all aspects of courage. Mental, social, spiritual, and intellectual courage are all required for strong, capable, competent, and complete leadership.

DON'T SUCCUMB TO ANALYSIS PARALYSIS . . .

As leaders, we're going to make mistakes. Absent a commitment to a philosophy like "Have courage, lead boldly," leaders sometimes fall into a trap of analysis paralysis, thinking, *I have to overthink it. I have to analyze everything over and over again before making a decision because I don't want to make a mistake.*

I wasn't always able to avoid this trap myself. For example, at Scott Air Force Base in Illinois, I worked with a senior leader who relied on me to provide good intelligence to support a decision that would impact the day-to-day operations of the base. As I mentioned, I was in my first senior leader position there, and I attended a preplanned 5 a.m. call to deliver my recommendation, as my team and I had researched and rehearsed. I had done the analysis, looked at the pertinent information, and talked to several experts, and I felt confident in the recommendation I was going to make. That morning, though, my boss and I fell into the analysis paralysis trap: "Let's call one more expert. Let's bring in one more researcher. Let's bring in one more piece of information before we make a final decision on a recommendation."

Sometimes a leader doesn't have the luxury of time to make those better-informed decisions. Often, they need to make the best-informed decision they can with the information available at the time, relying on some courage based on rational and relational confidence born across many years of experience and expertise. That morning, we had a decision window of sixty minutes, and while we were in analysis paralysis, we wound up eclipsing that window. This mattered, because it had an impact on people making decisions about their duty day—where they were going to be, when, and how they would apply their craft that day.

I learned a good lesson that morning about the importance of my tagline. Had I applied the courage to lead more boldly and to go ahead with our best recommendation as indicated by our prior work, the outcome would have been better. How much trust in our recommendation was lost because we missed our decision window?

. . . But Being "Brash" Doesn't Build Trust, Either

A leader wants to have the courage to lead boldly without being brash. I think being bold sometimes gets conflated with acting brashly, like the person who acts "large and in charge," barking orders and demanding compliance.

When a senior leader in a military unit gives an order—as long as it's not illegal, unethical, or immoral—it's supposed to be followed without question. This certainly makes sense in a battlefield environment. You can't have people second-guessing what the leader is asking them to do when an enemy is advancing.

But that's not what we're talking about here. Leading boldly (as opposed to behaving brashly) is recognizing that we're going for commitment, not simple compliance. There's a huge difference. Commitment is engagement in the direction we're providing, ownership of the decision that's been made, and follow-through to completion, motivated by faith in the leader and the plan. Even if team members don't agree 100 percent with the decision, because they trust the leader who is taking the courageous action, they're not simply complying with the order because they're required to. That trust is built over time, sometimes over a long period.

The military focus on following orders has a lot of similarities to a business context. If we're working on a manufacturing floor and we want our manufactured goods to be within tolerance levels to ensure a high-quality product, we need compliance. That's "crossing the T's and dotting the

I's," meeting all the specifications for the product. But many business decisions need to be made in a way that leads to commitment within the organization, based on the trust a leader can build in their decisions over time.

What I mean here is that we're not just taking action for action's sake; we're making wise decisions that people will commit to following because they trust us. A brash leader leads in the absence of that trust. If we as leaders are bold, with vision and voice, valuing the people around us, we'll generate commitment. Many years ago, I heard that trust is like a bank account. We deposit a nickel or a dime at a time, but when trust is lost, it's withdrawn five or ten dollars at a time. It's therefore incredibly important to keep the trust bank balance well positioned and positive.

GREAT LEADERS STAY HUMBLE

When we generate commitment, the outcome is usually much better than when we're just driving for compliance. I thought about the art of command, or top-level leadership, in this way: Humility is the single most important aspect of successful leadership because without it, we're susceptible to ethical drift.

I experienced this in my military career and have found it holds true in the private sector as well. For example, when a person is promoted from general manager to area vice president, managing vice president, or another nice private-sector title, they can very easily flip into this idea that they deserve it, they've earned it, or they're owed it: *Now that*

I'm in this new position of increased authority, I'm going to use it to make a name for myself and position myself for the next opportunity, they might think.

I thought about this very deliberately, particularly the last several times I was promoted in the Air Force and realized that as I became an executive leader, my responsibility set obviously became much greater and grander than before. There were going to be more eyes watching me, more ears listening to what I had to say. In some respects, it's like being a parent—our children watch everything we do, and hear everything we say, whether or not we realize it, and they will mimic the behaviors we display and demonstrate. Across my military career, even though no one said these exact words to me, it was really driven home that my responsibility was to be mindful that I was borrowing the rank I was given, but for a time, from the nation I served.

We can use that mindset to be thoughtful about the need for courage tempered with humility. We need to lead boldly but also to recognize that our leadership position is not about ourselves as individuals; it's about the team, the collective.

Our military uniforms don't always display our names, but they all have "US" on them. Throughout my Air Force leadership career, I tried to lean into this notion of US, not me or I. Just because I had the seat at the head of the table, the big corner office, or the title didn't mean it was about me. It was always about US executing what we needed to do in and for the organization.

ART AND SCIENCE

As I've learned by researching, reading, and learning extensively over the course of my career, there's certainly a lot of sound behavioral science about leadership: how people respond to leaders, hear our voices, see our vibrance, catch our vision, and respond to those things.

But there's also some art here. It's not just about figuring out some algorithm that gets people to commit to the things a leader is asking them to do. It's also about recognizing that the human aspect of leadership requires a certain artfulness. I often refer to "power skills"—your ability to communicate, engage with others, show empathy, and demonstrate high-value ethics, among others. Those skills comprise more of the art of influencing and moving our teammates to action. One specific way art is applied is beyond generating buy-in by setting an example; it's allowing our teams to find their own voice, vibrance, and vision. This is not about convincing people or applying science-based negotiating strategies, although that's necessary when resistance is high. It's about practicing consistent and clear interpersonal engagement that inspires people to commit to the goals, objectives, and desired outcomes as if the idea they're supporting were their own. It's about understanding the importance of interpersonal relationships. Here, art is not manipulation but modeling and maintaining trust and connecting on a personal level with those around us. The best outcomes flow from using both sound leadership science and aware artfulness to lead with courage and boldness, but without brashness or arrogance.

A number of years ago, it occurred to me that *arrogate* is the root word for *arrogance*. As a leader, if we try to arrogate, or to draw power to ourselves, it will lead to arrogance. It's really important for leaders at all levels, but certainly at the executive levels, to be very thoughtful about protecting themselves from those things.

Part of the art of leadership is having an accountability partner, somebody who will call us out if we're leaning too far into the power of our role. My wife is the person who has done that for me for decades. Sometimes she would say, "You check that rank at the door. When you come home, it doesn't matter. Here, you are a husband and father. Your roles and responsibilities here are not whatever that rank suggests." She helped me think deliberately about that, and not just at home. From time to time, she would call me out if she thought (probably rightly) that I was leaning a little too much into "Look at me, in this executive position, wearing this high rank!"

The need to show humility as a leader has a solid basis in science. Doing it, though, takes a little art.

DISRUPTION

Balancing between the behavioral science and the human art of connecting with people, a leader recognizes the need to find other people who live this idea of having courage and leading boldly—people who understand the power of going beyond simple compliance to engendering and energizing commitment. In the search for such people, leaders often look for those who demonstrate the ability to think outside the box.

A number of years ago, I engaged in a series of conversations with people in the Air Force and Space Force about the difference between people who are creative and those who are innovative. It became a really interesting exercise because it's common to conflate the two. My own analysis and study, from reading a wide variety of periodicals, papers, and polished books on the subject, indicate that creativity and innovation are not the same. Creativity brings something a little different or lovely or beautiful or artful without necessarily being disruptive. Innovation is disruptive.

A good example of an innovative disruption in technology was Apple's journey to the iPhone. As mentioned previously, Steve Jobs never planned to stop at the iPod, or even at the iTunes application. Those were innovations, and they required creative, out-of-the-box thinking by Apple personnel, but they were really gateways to Jobs's vision for the iPhone, which truly disrupted the market. Never before did people have a handheld device that enabled them to do essentially everything, from managing their calendar or financial transactions to buying stocks and securities, checking email, interacting on social media, messaging, reading the news, watching videos, taking photos with a high-resolution camera, and making phone calls. The iPhone was so disruptive, in a positive way, that it changed how every person with access to it perceived the world.

A leader like Steve Jobs knew he wasn't going to make everyone happy, and ice cream does make me happy. A leader cut from that cloth understands the difference between doing something that's beautiful and artful and doing something that's so disruptive, it positively changes an organization's mission and execution. In my second-to-last Air Force assignment—helping build the brand-new Space Force with my team—I worked very deliberately to create this same kind of disruptive force. To accomplish such a bold disruption, we needed (and had) a very small subset of humans inside the Department of the Air Force who had the right skills; physical, intellectual, emotional, and social courage; and willingness to step out boldly and do things differently. They were positive disruptors.

I remember having a conversation with a couple of more senior leaders that explored this thinking even further during my last assignment before retirement. We talked about whether there might be tens of thousands of professionals in the Air Force who are innovative, but that's not what the research revealed. A very small number of humans are truly innovative. My input and information met with some pushback and skepticism, but we had the data and detail available to prove that point. Establishing this new disruption required being careful about making sure that we didn't think just anybody with a good idea was innovative. Creative, yes. But innovative? Perhaps—even probably—not.

It's really important to understand the difference, especially when you're thinking about having courage, leading boldly, and moving your organization forward to that next iteration and ideation. Otherwise, to return to the entertainment industry analogy, you could become like Blockbuster Video, relegated to the dustbin of history, rather than like the next Netflix or Hulu or other highly successful, ever-evolving, streaming service.

* * *

Those four words—"Have courage, lead boldly"—have encapsulated so much of what was relevant and resonant in the last third of my Air Force career in executive roles. For me as a leader, they formed a great tagline and a great way to think about leadership on a continuous basis.

I'm grateful to General McDew for many things, not only for those four wonderful words but for taking the time to help me deeply develop and greatly grow as a leader. He did for me what great leaders always do: find ways to develop great leadership in others. They use what they've learned to invest in the next generation of leadership. That's the subject of our next chapter.

CHAPTER 6
TEACH AND TRUST

The difference between a politician and a statesman
is that a politician thinks about the next election,
while a statesman thinks about the next generation.

—James Freeman Clarke

Making an investment in the next generation of leaders is
one of a leader's most important responsibilities. In fact, for
many years now, I have thought it to be a leader's number
one responsibility, whether they find themselves at the front
end of an organization or in the C-suite. Whatever position
we occupy in an organization, if we're leaders, our number
one priority—our primary purpose and observable objective—is to develop other leaders. Here, the best leaders look
past the next cycle and into the farther future, into that next
leadership generation.

As we discussed in the previous chapter, a great leader is bold and courageous but stays humble. They naturally lean into using what they've learned and experienced to invest in the leaders coming up behind them.

It's been impressed upon me for a number of years that a leader is not successful if they're unable to teach others. By this, I don't mean that everything a person does at any leadership level is done to teach others how to fulfill that particular position. Rather, a good leader needs to be able to teach people to do new things.

As leaders, we have to lean into being teachers, mentors, and coaches. We're not necessarily the same thing to every person in our charge or within our leadership sphere, but we need to be actively teaching people. That goes beyond simply asking someone to do the things we say; it's about thinking like a role model and asking ourselves whether we're demonstrating the things we want others to do.

LEADERS SHOULD BE TEACHERS

When I was a freshman in college, I was taking a required calculus course, and I remember going into that first class session and learning the gentleman who was teaching the course was a retired US Navy nuclear engineer. *Well that's interesting*, I thought; I'd had some exposure to military people, but this was the first time I remember having a teacher at any level who'd had a prior military career.

I had no doubt that he understood calculus himself, particularly as a nuclear engineer, but I had every doubt that he could teach it to me. After the first week of classes, I wasn't grasping some of the concepts. I was a good student, so it wasn't like I didn't have some propensity toward math; I just couldn't relate to the way he was trying to teach differential equations. I went to his office hours at the first opportunity, and as I walked in, I knew that I wasn't alone in seeking extra help but also that I probably needed to drop his class and find a different professor. He held office hours in a classroom, as opposed to his actual office, and that classroom was standing room only. Every desk was filled, and the walls were lined with fellow classmates who were similarly trying to grasp what he was attempting to teach us.

Now, while that was an academic setting, even all those years ago, it taught me a little bit about the idea that if we want to lead and teach, we need to be able to communicate in a way that is effective for our students. For that reason, the way I tried to teach people wasn't the same for all of them.

For example, I had a troop who worked for me a number of years ago who was in a more senior role, and I had given this person a number of assignments that I wanted him to lead for the organization. He was struggling with the time commitments and quality standards I asked him to meet. It occurred to me that I wasn't teaching him what I needed him to do. It wasn't that I felt I should teach him how to do every single action or activity to fulfill a specific task or objective; rather, I realized I hadn't given him clarity in a way that he understood.

He joined me at a little four-person roundtable in my office, where I asked him what challenge I needed to address. Not that he was doing something wrong, but as his leader, what did I need to do to help him in a way that resonated with him? How did I need to adjust to instruct him, teach him, and entrust him to do the work?

I came to understand that I'd given him so many things to do all at once, it was overwhelming him. He didn't know where to start. In this case, I hadn't prioritized what was most important. So we went through a prioritization exercise, and I gave him some instructions: "Here's what I would like you to focus on, priority number one. Then here's the least important thing," and so forth. We worked through his assignments in this way, and I learned that I should go beyond assigning him work and teach him how to undertake the work in a way that he best understood.

After that, he was able to sift through the noise and focus on the things that were most important. Our relationship changed for the better, precisely because I had taken the time as a leader to understand that I needed to teach him differently from other teammates, and that was okay.

It also helped me think about this idea of developing other leaders by demonstrating the kinds of behaviors and actions I wanted them to do themselves, but I also realized there were things I had to get over. Returning to the discussion of humility from previous chapters, I needed to realize that my legacy wasn't about me. It wasn't about my reputation, my name, or the way I would be remembered (let alone memorialized for eons) after I'd left the position. No, as leaders, it's about thoroughly equipping the people who will remain after we're gone so that they won't need us.

I learned that, aside from just developing leaders as a primary objective, as a leader myself, I was not to worry at all about my legacy. I came to know that the greatest legacy I could leave behind in an organization was a team that could carry on at a very high level in my absence. That became my focus.

TEACH, AND THEN TRUST

It's not enough to make it incumbent on ourselves to teach people. The other side of the equation, when we're looking to develop the next generation of leaders, is to trust them.

While developing other leaders should be a leader's primary objective, and teaching is the important first step in that process, the most difficult thing for a leader to do is to give authority to those we teach. We have to trust them to make decisions and resist the instinct to make every decision ourselves.

Throughout my career, I've worked with, for, and around leaders who did not truly trust. I have replaced people in positions who did not demonstrate a level of trust. And let me be careful to say this is not an indictment of any one person. I was always very comfortable with giving my authority away. I operate well in what the US military first coined as "the VUCA environment"—volatile, uncertain, complex, and ambiguous. Early in my career, I became very comfortable with ambiguity, and so my tolerance for trusting people was much higher than perhaps most others'.

We have to recognize that we need to be deeply deliberate about developing others—we pour into them our experiences, expertise, and education. We share our own developmental journeys and find ways to instruct, inform, and illuminate things like confident decision-making, being a lifelong learner, and how to influence others. This requires us pouring effort and energy into them, being transparent about what we've learned over time, sharing our successes and failures with them, then trusting them to make decisions using tips, techniques, and tools we taught them to use.

Some leaders fall into the trap of thinking, *I'm more or less supposed to be Superman! I don't make mistakes. I make the right decisions all the time. I have some sort of superhuman ability to avoid ever making a mistake.* Many business leaders and behavioral scientists confirm that having this mindset, in and of itself, is a huge mistake. Lessons from failure resonate the most with people. If I had a dollar for every time I heard somebody say they've learned more from bad leaders or mistakes than from good leaders and successes, I'd be super wealthy. It's not that we can't learn from successes or from strong leaders, but the lessons that are likely to be more crystallized in our minds and more impactful in our memories come from failures and catastrophes.

I tried to be transparent about sharing mistakes that I made over the course of my career. I wasn't offering to self-immolate but I admitted I often made mistakes, which gives people the opportunity to learn and discern what I learned from those mistakes. We'll cover this in more detail in part III, and particularly in chapter 11. In shorter summary here, it's about just being transparent, and then being absolutely present.

LEAD PEOPLE WHERE THEY ARE

In part, this is why the book is titled *The Mission of Leadership*, because I believe the best leaders are the ones who are present, understanding that their leadership presence is central to their overall mission as leaders. They're out and about, engaging people, not being disruptive but finding ways to resonate, relate, communicate, and connect with people right where they are, even in this modern age with all these digital capabilities around us. Our mission as leaders is engaging people where they are.

When we think about the current work environment, there are six generations in the workforce. Six generations! It goes all the way back to what are now known as the traditionalists, the parents of the baby boomers. Yes, there are actually some traditionalists in various advanced ages at this point who are still working. Then we have the baby boomers, and then Gen X, Gen Y, Gen Z, and now Gen Alpha. Gen Alpha is the newest entrant and a smaller subset—teens who have started working jobs. Nevertheless, as leaders, we're likely to work with people from many different generations.

Recognizing this in my last several roles before retirement, for many years in my career, I would sit down with my direct reports and ask, among other questions, "How do you best communicate?" Some will say they need the analog one-on-one, face-to-face, voice-to-voice. Others, depending on their generation, might be more inclined to say, "Just text me." That doesn't work in every environment or for every situation, but just understanding how people are thinking about communication helped me to understand where and how to best engage them. Whether in person or in cyberspace, my mission was to reach them where they were so that I could teach them and so that they could learn I trusted them. I was willing, again, to have enough humility as a leader to say one size doesn't fit all and not require people to bend to my preferred communication style or platform.

I used analog methods, digital capabilities, or whatever it took to communicate with people where they were because I knew that while there would be some overlap in communication methods in different parts of my organization, I was trying to fill any gaps that might exist if I wasn't communicating in the space where that teammate was most likely to pick up the information. It was important to do whatever was necessary to be present. Again, I call this book *The Mission of Leadership* because I see leadership essentially as a mission field. I often refer to it as a "ministry of presence." Being good leaders, if not great leaders, is about conducting a ministry of presence. Do people see us? Do they know us? Do they hear from us? Do they connect with us? Do they trust us? Do they know we care about them? Do they know we know what they're accomplishing?

This goes back to a central question: Are the people we lead committed to or merely compliant with us? It's really hard to be committed to a leader if you've never seen them or heard from them, if you don't think they're interested in you, if they don't engage you, if they aren't teaching you, and if they haven't earned your trust.

TEACHERS KEEP LEARNING

Returning to the sturdy stool analogy shared in chapter 2, as leaders, we must be deliberate about developing ourselves and continuing in that growth mindset. There's always something more to learn, something more to know, and something more to do to be able to master ourselves. We can't just expect that people around us will continue to grow and groom their own capabilities and competencies if we're not doing the same.

Reaching our goals, as leaders, teachers, or organizations is the job. Given this, how we get to those goals really matters. We have to ask ourselves, *Are we looking at things both objectively and subjectively?* We might assume, because we sit down and have coffee with somebody and attempt to teach them, coach them, or provide mentorship, that we've accomplished our leadership mission. We need to know how that person is going to be most receptive to what we're trying to help them learn, but we also need a way to measure whether or not people are actually learning and growing. That goes back to trust—giving them the opportunity to make decisions. They might make mistakes, and that's okay as long as they learn from them.

As we lean into the growth mindset and learn more about leading as teachers, we have to watch out for the Dunning-Kruger effect, the trap of thinking you know more than you actually do because you've been successful in your position for a time (particularly if you have a longer career). Leaders have to guard against becoming intellectually incurious. As we rise in the leadership hierarchy, we need to ask more questions, not fewer. That's not to say we haven't gained additional expertise in areas, but we shouldn't assume we have all the answers just because we have experience in leadership positions, even, as in my case as I write this book, for more than three decades.

It would be foolish to think I have all the answers simply because I've successfully led in high-stakes, high-demand, high-risk environments for decades. Every time I walk into a situation, I know I don't have all of the answers. If I'm modeling the false notion that I have all the answers, but people around me continue to see me making mistakes, however big or small those mistakes may be, they're not going to trust me (or my decisions), and they're certainly not learning anything from me as a teacher.

We need to watch out for that in ourselves as well as in others. Throughout the arc of my military career, and now in the private sector, I've valued the leaders who poured their personal effort and energy into me as I was growing and helped me to learn and apply. I'm reminded of an old

Jewish idea: being "covered in the dust of the rabbi." As I understand it, this comes from the tradition of the Mishnah rabbis, teachers who had disciples or students around them. The statement goes "May you be covered in the dust of your rabbi" because in ancient times, the rabbi wouldn't just teach in a single synagogue. His students would follow him from village to village over dirt roads. Those who followed most closely would be covered in dust that the rabbi's sandals had kicked up—the symbol of a close and connected teacher-pupil relationship that led to deep learning.

In a more modern context, we're metaphorically covered in the dust of the rabbi when we're learning from a leader who's leaned into the mission of teaching and developing other leaders. I love this as a beautiful illustration of rabbinical teaching and leadership. As teaching leaders, are we allowing people to be that close to us? Are we getting so close to people that the things we know that could be valuable to them are in fact being passed on to them? Not actual dust, as with the character Pigpen from the *Peanuts* comic strip—but are they really learning what will be useful for them so that as they grow in their leadership capabilities, they can pass those things on to others in both word and deed?

One more important point: Just because a person isn't in a formal leadership position doesn't mean they aren't a formal leader. Some of the best leaders I can think of in my professional life weren't in positions of authority, but because of their powerful presence, competence, commitment, and courage, they were able to lead others around them. I've even been led from below (as I mentioned earlier, I learned the concept of the leadership constitution from a subordinate). I've worked with many teammates over the years, from whom I'm constantly learning. That brings us back to the idea of staying humble, never thinking that someone in a subordinate position to us or even in a position of less relative responsibility isn't also leading upward and across their own organizations. That kind of thinking could cause us to miss out on a lot of important lessons as leaders.

* * *

When I was promoted to Brigadier General, the director of Air Force Manpower, Personnel, and Services (basically, the chief human capital and wellness officer for the US Air Force), Lieutenant General Brian Kelly, declared at my promotion ceremony that I had "a passel of mentors." It was absolutely true—I benefited mightily, from my very first job in the Air Force all the way through my current professional, post–Air Force life, from men and women who have deliberately and deeply taught me to be a better leader. They taught me to make better decisions, to constantly be learning, and to lean into being a leader myself. Every one of them trusted me even when I didn't think I had the capacity to make the best or brightest decisions at the time.

"Teach and trust" is right at the core of who I am as a leader. Again, my legacy is developing other leaders, not trying to be memorialized on a plaque in a US Air Force building somewhere in the world.

I'd rather my name be carved in the hearts of leaders I've helped to develop than on any wall, anywhere.

CHAPTER 7
MOMENTS THAT MATTER

Carve your name on hearts, not on marble.

—Charles Spurgeon

It's simple human nature that we can perceive any of the things that happen in our lives—small, medium, or large—as "moments that matter." These are the events that move us to action. They help us see ourselves in a different way. They help connect us to one another.

Early in my Air Force career, I had the opportunity to work for Mr. Arthur Myers. He was a Senior Executive Service civilian (a two-star general officer equivalent at that time) in the US Air Force, serving as the director of what we call Morale, Welfare, and Recreation. There are a huge number of things in that particular portfolio (akin to a multinational business conglomerate of, at the time, more than

$4 billion in annual revenue), and Mr. Myers brought me onto his staff during my first of three assignments covering nearly ten years at the Pentagon.

Arthur Myers was the single most important and impactful mentor I had across the entire arc of my Air Force career, so much so that when the time came for my promotion to full-bird colonel, I asked him to officiate that ceremony, and he did. He later attended my promotion to Brigadier General, and when I retired from the Air Force, he presented my retirement medal to me. This just illustrates not only how important that leader was to me personally but also how he impacted me professionally. He modeled time and again what Dr. Ken Blanchard wrote about decades ago in his book *The One Minute Manager* about being present around the organization, and he was really attuned to catching people doing things right. His mission was leadership.

I learned early on that sometimes leaders can get too focused on mistakes. To be clear, leaders can't just walk past problems or missteps; we need to focus on them. That said, a good leader doesn't make errors the thing on which they spend the most time. Instead, they find people doing things well. And they highlight it very visibly.

Mr. Myers did a lot of that during the year I worked for him. He was out and about in the organization, not trying to get in the way of our work but doing simple check-ins and, most of all, encouraging and engaging us when things were going well.

One of the techniques he used, which blew me away, I observed during the holiday season that year. He handwrote a letter to every person on his immediate staff—several dozen people. A couple of decades later, I still have the letter he wrote to me because it was so impactful to me that he took the time to write it.

First of all, he has beautiful penmanship. More importantly, he didn't just write me a generic letter: "Happy holidays, enjoy Christmas with your family," that sort of thing—which would've been nice enough. Instead, he took the time to deliberately detail some of the things I had accomplished as a part of his team.

His salutation consisted of something he has always given and still does today: encouragement. Over the decades since, every single time we've exchanged emails or messages, it's been the same. I come away from those exchanges having usually learned something and being very appreciative that he leaned into me individually—not just a member of his team but me personally. He modeled, mentored, and molded a great many things in me beyond that note.

While I was on his team, he asked me to take an Air Force–wide, influential leadership role, creating and curating key mechanisms and methods of supporting our junior officers (of which I was one at the time—a Captain, a mid-level manager). Every couple of months, I went to our schoolhouse, where we trained all officers in our specific career field or specialty, to share what we were deliberately doing on their behalf. We were trying to make them better young leaders, teaching and trusting them to make decisions all across the Air Force. One of my trips happened to coincide with a visit to the schoolhouse by Mr. Myers and his executive officer, Captain Brian Rendell (now a retired Colonel). I shared the nature of the executive officer post in chapter 2; I held the same position for Colonel Peggy Shaw.

The morning we were flying from Washington Reagan National Airport to Cincinnati, Ohio, Mr. Myers and I were booked on the same flights. I knew that beforehand and looked forward to spending some extra time in the company of this incredible, impressive leader. When we connected at the airport, there were the usual greetings and small talk. Then he handed me a brown paper lunch bag. I opened it to find he had made me a sandwich and added a banana and a cookie to the bag. Since we had to drive from Cincinnati to Dayton without stopping for lunch to make our briefing times that afternoon, this two-star-general-equivalent C-suite leader had personally made me lunch. He was, in military terms, six layers superior to me. In corporate parlance, this was akin to a C-suite executive packing a lunch for a district manager as they traveled together. It was a moment that mattered. With that small act, he demonstrated humility and humanity, and he helped me know that was the kind of leader I wanted to be. I wanted to emulate and embody that selflessness and self-assurance. I've endeavored to do the same in the decades since.

Everyone Wants Feedback

These two experiences, among countless others, helped me understand that every person wants feedback, interaction, and impact from their leaders. They may not ask for it, but they want it.

It's also important to understand the manner or method or mode of feedback that is most impactful for a person. Leadership practitioners know that some people prefer public praise and pronouncements, while others thrive on quiet, private exchanges: "Shake my hand, look me in the eye, and say, 'Thank you. You did a good job.'" Leaders need to become attuned and attenuated to the engagement preferences of those they lead and then (as discussed in the previous chapter) meet them where they are to give them that feedback.

I also learned that these moments aggregate. As I mentioned, for decades in our communications, Mr. Myers has continued to encourage me and to give me thoughtfulness—and that has a powerful impact on me to this day. Sometimes his email was just a couple of sentences, but when you take all of those things together, the sum is much greater than the parts.

When I was entering my first mid-level management job in the Air Force, he took the time to teach and encourage me again. This was a position for which Mr. Myers had directly intervened to help me attain (and it also blew me away to know that he was that engaged in my professional development, opening up purposeful pathways for my continued growth even before I went to that role). He said, "You need to be a prolific writer here." He didn't mean I needed to be writing op-eds or huge missives, or email after email, and shotgunning things out to the entire team. He went on to explain: "You have to take time to handwrite thank-you cards to people." Another example was the annual letter that he wrote to every person on his staff. I didn't need him to point out that those little things really matter and go an enormous way if leaders take the time to do them.

There's the power of humility again. Instead of just shotgunning an email or, these days, shooting off an email we didn't even write consisting of an AI-generated script manufactured from a quick prompt, leaders need to sit down and deliberately take the time to handwrite cards or letters.

"This is a lost art," Mr. Myers said. "People don't handwrite cards and notes in the same way they once did because we live in a digital age now. It's easy to simply shoot a text, fire off an email, or find some other quick method of communication." Some people like to do little videos and send those to you. Those also matter, and they might be the way some people could best consume the information. But taking time to handwrite messages and recognizing the power of those small things will have outsized impacts.

We have to do what it takes to make sure people understand that we care about them. Remember what John C. Maxwell said: "People don't care how much you know until they know how much you care." From Myers to Maxwell, this was a powerful lesson for me.

Speaking of alliteration, of which I'm a big fan (can you tell?), the habit I formed focused on what I called "babies, birthdays, and big deals."

I shared with my teammates that anytime somebody inside my organization had a baby, I wanted to know because I was going to handwrite a congratulatory card. And if they could get me the baby's name and some of the particulars without overly prying into people's private lives, I would include some of that intelligence in my note as well. "Congratulations on the birth of Johnny! I understand he's nineteen and a half inches long, weighs eight and a half pounds, and already has a full head of hair," I'd write. Whatever the details were, I mentioned them to make it personal to them.

For years, I handwrote birthday cards to all the key leaders on my teams, and in some cases when the teams were about 50 people, it was easy enough for me to write a card to every single one on their birthday. In other instances, when I was leading 1,500 people or even more than 3,000, it was basically impossible to write that many, so I had a "cutoff." But scores to hundreds of people in those organizations received handwritten cards from me on their birthdays.

Then there were the "big deals." If somebody graduated from college, attained a certain certification, had been a distinguished graduate from a program, won a major award, got married, or had another big thing happening in their life, I wanted to know about it so I could handwrite cards to them. Unlike birthday cards, I had no cutoff for how many of these cards I would write.

The babies, birthdays, and big deals were a big deal to me. Yes, it took time, but I wanted to engage with people by writing those notes. For some major events (an air show or graduation at the Air Force Academy, for example), there were usually hundreds and hundreds of people who would have been engaged in making that happen. There were many nights I came home and handwrote birthday or baby notes at the dinner table because I was that invested in it.

While I served as Tenth Airbase wing and installation commander (essentially, as the "mayor" of that "city") at the United States Air Force Academy, we had a dozen air-show-sized events every year, from six home football games to the largest and most important annual event—graduation. Those events supported tens of thousands of guests. It was, in some respects, like holding a day-long county fair. There is an incredible number of moving parts to manage when executing each of these events. I wrote thousands of letters over the couple of years I was at the Academy. Most were form letters, but I endeavored to add something handwritten and personal to every single thank-you letter. It may have been a standard "You did these things, thank you for that, we appreciate your support." But at the bottom, I would put a little note thanking them for doing an excellent job.

In an organization of more than 3,000 people, the likelihood I would remember every single name was low. I do remember faces but not always names. In any event, if the letter was going to somebody I knew personally or remembered having met, I wrote a bit more so they would know I wasn't simply affixing my signature to a form letter. I wanted to demonstrate some deliberateness and show that I had put some thought into connecting and trying to communicate how much I appreciated their work. It was also important that I had their "go-by name" correct. We all know people who, for example, use their middle name rather than their first name. Others use a nickname that I wouldn't know by reading their formal name. A technique almost every military leader I know uses is to run a single pen line across the printed name on these pro forma thank-you notes and handwrite the person's go-by name above that line. My staff worked to ensure that I handwrote "Cristina" or "Chrissy" rather than "Kristina" or "Krissi." Those little things took only a few seconds but demonstrated that I had personally touched every single letter rather than just whipping my signature across the bottom with no thought for the person it addressed. Details always matter. The little moments matter.

As leaders, we have to be absolutely consistent as we undertake these kinds of efforts. Unsurprisingly, the people who are affected by them will share their experiences with others: "Hey, I got a note from the leader on my college graduation. Not only did she handwrite it, but she got some of the details that I wouldn't have thought she knew about." We've demonstrated a little more interest in connecting right where that person is. But if we stop doing it or if we're inconsistent, that will also get out, and it could create the impression that we care about only certain segments or subgroups as opposed to treating everybody with the same consistent care.

DON'T DO IT FOR THE APPLAUSE

Sometimes we get to "hear the applause," but that's not why we do things like this in leadership. We do them because they're the right things to do. It's about making human connections, demonstrating that we care no matter how much we actually know, and applying Maxwell's maxim from above.

A good leader is willing to engage people, and not just by writing letters. The handwritten notes are just part of a leader's ministry of presence or the mission of leadership— being where people are, engaging them, hearing their stories, and simply trying to connect and communicate with them.

For many years as a leader, I got to know people's stories partly by conducting quarterly commander's calls. In a business context, you could think of these as a sort of all-call, when the CEO has a chance to get on a call with the entire company. Jeff Bezos famously did this at Amazon when he was still running the ship there, and organizations that I work in now do the same thing on a routine basis.

To prepare for my commander's calls, which were live events or extensive video conferences, I learned stories from people. Then I shared their stories during those quarterly calls. I'm sure people didn't necessarily understand why their picture had been taken one day, sort of at random. But during the commander's call, there I was in front of 600, or 1,500, or even several thousand people, and that picture would pop up on the screen. I would then spend a couple minutes talking about something great we had caught that person doing (to recall the notion of "catching people doing things right," as proposed by Dr. Blanchard and practiced by Mr. Myers). I found this created powerful connections and clearly showed the leader was paying attention to things that were happening three to six layers down in the organization.

To distribute that positive impact, I was always careful to balance the types of people I put on the screen. We included people from disparate parts of the organization to ensure that highlights and recognition were wide and varied. We also ensured we had a good mix of officers, enlisted, and civilian personnel.

At one of these quarterly all-calls, I had encouraged the people around me to reach for things they wanted to accomplish. Some of their goals were hard to achieve, but I exhorted them not to sell themselves short of their big dreams or desires, either personally or professionally. Take that moon shot or loon shot, I told them. A couple of years after I left the Air Force Academy, I was back in the Pentagon for my third, and last, assignment in the building, and I got an email from a person whose name I didn't recognize. I usually scan quickly to make sure it's not a phishing expedition or other nefarious message. But this email was from someone I had worked with, who shared that I had encouraged them during one of those Air Force Academy commander's calls when I was sharing stories. It had inspired them to go back to school, finish their bachelor's and master's degrees, and join the FBI.

I honestly don't know if I could pick that person out of a crowd and tell you who she was, but her email floored me. I read it easily a dozen times, amazed that something simple I had said resonated and rang so true for her. Just giving some encouragement and challenging people to challenge themselves can be the impetus for them to start down a pathway they've long desired to pursue. That was a moment that mattered, and I hadn't even realized it at the time.

Similarly, while at the Air Force Academy, I had a responsibility to review military members' applications for retirement or separation. One such application came across my desk, and as I read through it, something just didn't sit right with me. This turned out to be an example of being engaged in a moment that matters instead of just looking at every administrative task that comes across the desk without curiosity, care, or questioning. I wanted to be thoughtful about going beyond just signing off on that application, because it had been impressed upon me years earlier that a signature is sacrosanct. No one can take your reputation from you, but you can give it away. For that reason, it was important for me to make sure that I didn't just do pass-through with things that were having a real impact on people's lives. Retiring or separating from the military, from wearing the uniform, is a significant decision.

As I looked at the application, I recognized a superstar performer—exactly the kind of young, enlisted, non-commissioned officer (frontline leader) I knew we needed to keep in the Air Force. He had advanced to his current rank very quickly. In fact, there was no faster way to reach it. He was also completing his last course for his undergraduate degree. In any other circumstance, he was the kind of young leader I might have put forward, or even pushed forward, to get an officer's commission, as my passel of mentors had pushed me to do very early in my career. In short, this was a person the Air Force really didn't want to lose.

I learned that he wanted to continue serving, but his wife had a medical condition that required her to stay below 3,000 feet of elevation. The symptoms of this particular medical malady were exacerbated at altitude, and the Air Force Academy is more than 6,000 feet above sea level.

She was having some significant struggles with her condition, but the Air Force, like many big bureaucratic organizations, didn't see this airman as an individual. It saw him as another package to be processed three different times. He asked for any remedies available to him and his family. The first two times he asked, he was turned down only because he had used the wrong program application process. The third time, the person who reviewed his package was likely not mal-intended but simply read the policies without taking an extra thirty seconds to get to a moment that mattered. The reviewer indicated that because a uniform-wearing military physician hadn't signed off on his request, the package couldn't be actioned. It turned out that the physician who was best at diagnosing and treating this rare medical condition was a non-military-affiliated civilian because it was an acute specialty we didn't have available inside the Air Force. In fact, this person's physician was the best specialist in the state of Colorado and happened to practice just a few miles from the Air Force Academy.

It took me just a few minutes to dig into the issue and recognize there was a way to remedy it quickly. I called the Air Force Personnel Center, which is essentially the headquarters for most Air Force human resource functions. I shared the story, and within a couple of days, we were able to get that developing leader and his family reassigned to an Air Force base near his wife's lower-altitude hometown.

We kept that promising young man in the Air Force.

Now, I never met this airman. He didn't work for me. He was just stationed on the installation. Nevertheless, I was able to recognize a moment that could really matter. Just by engaging for a few minutes, I knew we could change that young man's direction. He chose to continue serving in uniform, which was a huge win for the Air Force and, more broadly, for our nation.

That story serves as an exceptional example of the power of being on the lookout for moments that matter.

If we just take the time as leaders to invest in people, we might come across something only a leader can do that really matters. We must invest that time even if we don't get feedback or hear the applause.

I called the airman after we worked out his transfer and told him how it had happened. He thanked me. To this day, that's the only conversation I've ever had with him. I know, though, that what we did for him mattered and changed not only his life but, much more importantly, that of his family.

* * *

I've had lots of mentors over the course of my career, and I always remember Mr. Myers when I think of the power of moments that matter. Once more, he was the most impactful civilian mentor I've ever had. He served a full uniformed career in the military prior to becoming a civilian military leader and C-suite executive. He was always looking at me as a person—at my character, competence, capability, and potential. One of my mentors from high school, to whom I'm still connected, said, "You shouldn't be afraid to sow the seeds even though you may never see the harvest. A harvest will come if you take the time to plant and water." I learned many great lessons from Arthur Myers and from the other leaders who took the time to invest in me, and one of the greatest of those lessons was about these moments that matter.

We won't always get feedback, and we won't always know what impact those moments have had. Nevertheless, as leaders, it's imperative that we lean in and work on moments that matter. Mr. Myers's name is carved on my heart. I hope others think the same about me. That would be the greatest testament to what I've attempted to accomplish for decades.

Some lessons you can learn only by working with great leaders and mentors who take an invested interest in you. You can also learn a lot about leadership by simply reading what great leaders have taken the time to write. That's the subject of our next chapter.

CHAPTER 8
LEADERS ARE READERS

To succeed in this world,
you have to change all the time.

—Sam Walton

This may be one of my favorite topics. Not that the other areas of leadership we cover in the book aren't important to me, but this is perhaps the one area in which people who know me best would most likely expect me to dive into and discuss.

In the summer of 2012, I moved from Washington, DC, after completing my second tour of duty at the Pentagon, to Cambridge, Massachusetts, where I became a national security fellow at Harvard's Kennedy School of Government. This is a position similar to a university research fellowship. My primary responsibilities were to listen to, work with, and learn from some of the world's foremost experts in geo-politics, policymaking, good governance, and much more. Many of those professors and professionals sharpened and solidified my ability to think at strategic levels. Many of them continue inspiring generational strategic leadership thinking. Among them are professors and practitioners with whom I directly interacted and engaged, and from whom I learned: Graham Allison, Joseph S. Nye (rest in peace), Meghan L. O'Sullivan, Pippa Norris, Swanee Hunt, Robert D. Blackwill, David Sanger, Nicholas Burns, David Gergen, and many others.

We focused on unlocking and understanding science-based politics, polities, and policies—not politics in a negative sense but the science behind how politics and policies work and research into which policies of federal and executive governance across the globe work best.

The National Security Fellows Program at Harvard University's John F. Kennedy School of Government is described as:

> "a closed-enrollment program that offers a ten-month postgraduate research fellowship for US military officers and government civilian officials from the intelligence community who show promise of rising to the most challenging lead-ership positions in their organizations. Selection for this program is done by the respective military services and agencies.

National security fellows study a wide range of strategic public management and security issues. They belong to a fellowship community that brings other practitioners, such as politicians, journalists, diplomats, and educators, to Harvard. After they leave Cambridge, they continue to take part in a variety of events organized regularly for alumni of the Kennedy School.

Fellows pursue group research projects and write a paper aimed at senior policymakers; audit classes at Harvard, Massachusetts Institute of Technology (MIT), and the Fletcher School at Tufts University; participate in the National Security Fellows Executive Program; attend guest speaker seminars hosted by the National Security Program and other groups around Harvard, MIT, and the Fletcher School; and participate in working groups associated with Harvard's various research centers and the national security studies programs at the Fletcher School and MIT."

For me, it was an opportunity to take the uniform off for an academic year and soak in a rigorous learning and leadership development environment. The Air Force has a high regard for these kinds of fellowships, particularly at civilian institutions, and certainly at one as world-renowned as Harvard. These are opportunities for military leaders to challenge the way we see the world and how we might impact and influence it. They aren't meant to move us in a different direction but to help us move beyond what General David Petraeus called "the cloister." (General Petraeus happens to have a PhD from Princeton University, so he knows a little bit about being an academic in addition to being a truly historic four-star general in the US Army.)

It was importantly impressed upon me that I shouldn't just use that year to refresh, recharge, and reinvigorate myself as I was poised to move into the executive ranks of the Air Force. Instead, I needed to use it to reframe, refocus, and reshape my ability to think strategically.

During my year at Harvard, I read thirty-two books and somewhere north of ten thousand pages of other content, from short pieces of several paragraphs or one-page op-eds to doctoral dissertations of hundreds of pages. I spent that year consuming, cataloging, and categorizing that information. The point, though, isn't how many pages I turned. It's the need I felt to accelerate my learning, not just about military things but also all the other connective things that I would need to be really thoughtful about as an executive-level leader in the Air Force. These were things like diplomacy, economics, and information—I had to learn to focus on all four instruments of national power and not just the military instrument.

I tried to be open-minded about ingesting information from different sources to improve the way I was likely to make decisions in strategic leadership roles. I was taking a different approach from anything I'd done before, recognizing that reading was good, but reading to apply was more important. President Harry S. Truman wrote, "Not all readers are leaders, but all leaders are readers." My key takeaway from that quote is that if you're going to lead effectively, you have to be "greedy and giddy about learning," and you have to be listening and leaning into what the best leaders have said.

We previously discussed the Dunning-Kruger effect, the dangerous false belief that reaching a high position or post makes someone the expert or means they have all the answers. In fact, the reverse is likely true. As we climb the leadership ladder, the number of things for which we're likely to have to make decisions increases, and the decisions themselves become larger and larger. The only way to be prepared for that is to continue reading and learning and to maintain a strong growth mindset—one of the legs in the sturdy stool from chapter 2.

The Air Force was sending me purposely to this world-class institution so I could understand things like cultural context, content, and nuance, things that maybe I didn't fully understand before. I needed to understand why people around the world think the way they do, why they act or respond the way they do, and how different concepts fit together in an overall strategic landscape.

By the time I finished my one-year fellowship in the summer of 2013 and became an alumnus of such an august institution as Harvard, a number of people with whom I'd shared that opportunity said, "Wow! It's pretty amazing that you had the opportunity to go there." I might be slightly modest, but the reality is the Air Force got me in there. I don't know if I would've gotten in on my own based on my prior academic pedigree, which was super solid, but I did learn from the experience. I had a marvelous time of self-discovery, self-learning, and soaking up the people with whom I was in contact, along with all the resources and connections that were available to me at that institution.

When I moved on from Harvard, I realized it wasn't good enough just to read. I wouldn't say that I've been a voracious reader all my life, but I grew up in a household where reading mattered. My father has an undergraduate degree in journalism, which you could say is both good and bad—Dad read pretty much everything I wrote all the way up until I was a freshman or sophomore in college, when I was commuting to campus from home. Up to then, he was still reading my papers and editing them, which could be painful at times. But even then, I recognized it's good to have somebody push you to sharpen your own thinking about things.

As a leader, it isn't enough just to lean into reading. I realized I also need to share with those around me what I was reading and its application. I didn't necessarily need to send a link to every article I was reading or information about every book I had touched, but it was important to share with the people around me. This goes back to the idea of teaching and trusting—I needed to model the behavior I wanted to see in others.

When I got to my next assignment after my year at the Kennedy School, I started what I called the Leaders Are Readers column. Initially I was producing that column every week, and each edition included eight to twelve articles I had read the previous week. I shared links to the articles along with some basic details about the information they contained, how that information mattered, and why it applied to the work we were doing.

After producing Leaders Are Readers for a couple years, I moved into a more executive role and realized it wouldn't be possible to keep doing the column every week. I turned it into a monthly product, which I still produce and provide to this day, a dozen years after my deep educational experience at the Kennedy School.

My thought was that even if no one learned anything from what I was sharing, it would still be useful for me because of how much I learned by engaging in the exercise. There's also a very interesting psychological phenomenon at play: I've received really good feedback over the years, and people share their own learning, such as books, articles, and podcasts or programs they think I might find interesting or illuminating. The stack of books that people have recommended to me sits on the bookshelf in my home office and in my Amazon wish list or save-for-later list, and I'll probably never get to all of them, but the conversations and communications have made it worthwhile either way.

I also post the column on my LinkedIn account, usually on the last Monday of every month. It helps me be accountable to continue the effort. I don't know how long I'll do it, but I know that while I continue to work full-time, I'll want to continue learning and gathering more information and intelligence that can be useful to the people I serve in my various roles.

I've also learned that it's important to give people an attribution when I share a book or article they recommended to me, for two reasons. I want them to know, first, that I actually read the material they sent me, and second, if it was something I found impactful or insightful, that I'm passing it on to others. As I think my dad would say, as a journalist, you need to attribute the source. I try to be consistent about that. I add a simple phrase to the column, a "hat tip" to the person who sent me the information. It encourages continued engagement, not just with what I publish every month but as an opportunity to make the column a two-way street. People know that if they share something they found insightful or informational, it may find its way into a column seen by, in some months, thousands of people. That's a great opportunity.

Another practice I put in place years before I retired from the Air Force, which I continue today, is to mark off thirty minutes on my professional calendar, usually at the beginning of the day, to read. Being completely transparent, I don't always use that thirty-minute slot. Sometimes it's not thirty minutes. Some days I take maybe five or ten minutes to read a couple of quick thought pieces and move on, depending on what's happening that day. But the point is that men and women on my team knew I was doing this. That was important, not just because they knew I was publishing the Leaders Are Readers missive but also because they knew I purposed time during my day to do the reading. That gave them permission to do the same.

I was modeling the idea that, while you can't read all day and you have to attend to your day-to-day responsibilities, you can do what I do: Block out time to nourish your own growth mindset by reading. My calendar was publicly available, and it still is. People knew that I had put this item on my own calendar and that I would pay them to do the same. If a person spent thirty minutes reading sometime in their day, that was fine by me, and I wanted to hear from them. I wasn't looking to do some sort of status check, but I wanted them to know it was okay.

As we discussed in chapter 6, there's both purpose and power in modeling the behaviors we want others to emulate. As I described, it's a little like being a parent, knowing our children pay very close attention to what we do and say, whether or not we notice they're doing it. I don't mean to suggest our team members are children, but the analogy holds: People are watching what we're doing as leaders. Therefore, if I demonstrated that I was spending time reading, changing all the time as Sam Walton shared at the top of this chapter, my teammates knew I took it seriously. When I shared things with them—not everything, but some of the things I was reading—they knew I was doing what I said I was doing, and I was giving something back to them.

Many, if not most, of the people around us will never respond to anything we share with them from our reading practice. That's okay. As leaders, we need to have courage, lead boldly, and do it anyway.

* * *

Reading should be a routine practice for any leader, as should be sharing what we've read and why the material matters to our team's work. When we maintain that practice, we're connecting with people in yet another way and teaching them. We're trusting them with our inner thoughts, especially if we share those thoughts openly, as I try to do in my Leaders Are Readers column.

I share what I'm thinking about what I've read, how I've applied it, and what has or hasn't worked.

If a daily reading/sharing practice doesn't work for you, perhaps you might try three days a week or even once weekly. Regardless of periodicity, it's important that leaders stay engaged in a continuous effort of learning, reading, sharing, and growing.

In essence, communicating with people—by sharing what we've read and learned through our own leadership journeys, for example—is what leadership is. For that reason, the best leaders are always thoughtful about the words they choose in both written and verbal communication. The purpose, promise, and power of words is the subject of our next exploration.

CHAPTER 9
WORD WISE

The power of the tongue is often disregarded. Be careful
what you say, and how you say it. Use your words to
inspire and encourage others, not to discourage and
stifle their growth. Your words are powerful.
Please choose them wisely.

—June Archer

Growing up with a father who had a degree in journalism, over time, I learned to emphasize the practice of carefully choosing words, in both written and oral communication.

As I mentioned, for most of my high school days, and certainly into the first couple of years of college when I was commuting from my dad's house to campus, he read all my research papers, pulled out the red pen, and marked up the documents, probably the same way any journalist or copy editor would. I'm just picturing the old *Washington Post* days when everything was done by longhand and typewriter as opposed to digitally. At any rate, it deliberately drove into me early in my life, in my formative years, to be thoughtful about the words I used, the construction of sentences, and the best way to communicate, regardless of form or format.

While I was in high school, I had the opportunity to participate in Junior Achievement. It typically pairs high school kids with professionals and entrepreneurs from either for-profit or nonprofit organizations to help the kids develop an entrepreneurial spirit, think about how they might bring a service or good to market, and consider all the things they would need to do to successfully sell it.

I was in the spring semester of my sophomore year, and our Junior Achievement project was to produce a newspaper. We worked with local print newspaper professionals at the time, both those who wrote editorial and opinion pieces and marketing professionals. One of our key instructors worked in marketing for my local hometown newspaper. We didn't just write articles; we also attempted to sell advertising space to local businesses.

I wouldn't suggest I had really mastered my words at that point, but I learned a lot through that experience about what it takes to write things that resonate with people. On the ad sales side, that semester, I was the highest seller. I was awarded a scholarship for a Dale Carnegie course in public speaking and effective relations.

WORDS THAT STAND THE TEST OF TIME

At that time, I hadn't heard of Dale Carnegie. Now, of course, I know that one of his most well-known books, *How to Win Friends and Influence People*, has sold somewhere north of thirty million copies. That book is now a good solid century old, but when it comes to communicating, I don't think all that much has changed. Some of the media we use are certainly different. When I was in high school, we were only getting into the first computer labs; today most students wander around with smart devices in their pockets. Some don't even get issued textbooks anymore.

I attended that Dale Carnegie course over the summer before my junior high school year, though I wasn't good at public speaking and didn't enjoy it. Like most people, I had a bit, or a bunch, of fear of it (I wouldn't necessarily say panic, but certainly fear). Nevertheless, I leaned into it and learned from that course.

My dad, of course, understood who Dale Carnegie was. We were issued a couple of Carnegie's books, and we worked through them. The entire premise of the course was to help us become better at communicating and connecting, more thoughtful about our words, and more effective in engaging people.

That course helped drive home for me the true power of communicating: the art of being a capable and captivating communicator and how truly important that is to leading people. I learned how to express what I value and to let my character, competence, commitment, and dedication and devotion to those around me come through. Whether it was in high school, college, or professional work environments, working with my fellow students and colleagues on projects, it was about becoming more effective as a communicator in both written and verbal contexts.

I learned a tremendous amount from that course, and I was awarded as the most improved public speaker over the course of the program. It was really impactful and important for me because it demonstrated that, as with most anything else, when we put in the time, effort, and energy to get better, we will. It gave me a lot more confidence, particularly as I became a young working professional, to review the things I learned in that course and apply them, first in my academic career and later in my professional career.

GREAT LEADERS ARE STRONG COMMUNICATORS

Communication skills become ever more important as our leadership journeys take us from the frontlines of the organization to the C-suite and beyond. That communication capability needs to be able to be transmitted across the entire organization. Throughout my career, I met many leaders who weren't really effective at communicating verbally and/or through the written word. I leaned into making strong communication a part of my leadership brand and worked to be a capable and (hopefully) captivating communicator. By "captivating," I don't mean that I'm Shakespearean or that people will always listen to me and come away saying

"Wow" or being inspired; rather, I aim to clearly articulate the things I hope for my team or those around me to advance and accomplish.

I focused on making communication something I was good at, and I put in the time and effort to continue improving. To this day, I try to be very thoughtful about the words I send out, whether I write them or speak them.

I worked with a friend at the Air Force Academy. We had gone to high school together and then wound up serving full careers in the US Air Force. It wasn't until his last assignment, my third-to-last assignment, a quarter-century later, that we had the opportunity to work together at the same installation. We nevertheless stayed connected over the years, and I remember him telling me as he was retiring that he felt like every time he heard me speak publicly, I didn't waste a word, and the things I presented really connected with the audience.

I took that to heart. I really appreciated it because, at least in this instance, I knew there was one human being who saw that I put a lot of effort into the way I was communicating with people.

Being thoughtful about our words is important across the variety of different ways leaders communicate daily, even in simple emails. I'm not suggesting I needed to overthink every email I wrote, to go back and review it over and over again. The emails that were giving instruction, though, or that were more than just "Thank you for sending me that information," I did take the time to write well. To use an old carpenter's adage, I wanted to be able to "measure twice and cut once," and not only when it came to day-to-day messages.

For example, in various leadership roles, I wrote messages about Memorial Day, the Fourth of July, or Veterans Day, or I put together holiday messages to send to my teams. Often I wrote those messages days or even weeks in advance so I could go back and refine them and provide something that would connect or deeply resonate with whoever was reading them.

Similarly, there were many official ceremonies in which I needed to take part. Some were as simple as a quarterly awards event, for which I spent a lot of time learning about the men and women we were highlighting and congratulating (not just those who won the awards but all the nominees). I made it a point over the last third of my Air Force career to learn "the names and numbers." When I led those events, I would communicate a meaningful message. I didn't just say something like "Hey, everybody did a great job this quarter, and we're going to highlight the winners!" I tried to make every nominee feel like they had won. That meant I needed to put time and effort into these things. I always recounted and recalled in depth the data and details to show I was in the particulars, not just glad-handing nominees and winners. It demonstrated that I was not a casual observer but a consumer of the great things people had accomplished. Winners and nominees knew I had consumed and considered the work of each and every one of them during that award period.

Usually, when I speak publicly, I don't use notes. This is another level of preparation I learned through the Dale Carnegie course—not to try to memorize everything word-for-word, because that's often a recipe for getting lost and falling apart mid-sentence. Instead, I train myself to find the "hooks" in my public comments. In the award ceremonies, I often used a number, a quote, or an alliterative phrase—something to help me walk through what I was trying to convey to the men and women to whom I was speaking. Even if they didn't remember anything in particular I had said, I wanted to make sure they felt good about the time they had spent with me and that they understood I was putting in the effort. (In Appendices B–D, I share my writing and communications to give examples of my efforts at being disciplined and deliberate in my verbal and written communications.)

As I mentioned, a military leader has to lead official ceremonies with some regularity. These are events like rank or grade promotions, retirements, and change-of-command ceremonies (when a new leader takes charge). It occurred to me early in my career that, in these ceremonies, most every leader seemed to follow the same script. They typically looked up the person or persons involved in the ceremony, read their official biographies or personnel records (like annual appraisals), and then recited what they had done: "This person started off in this job, then went to this job, then went to this job, and along the way, they accomplished this at this job, that at that job," and so on. At some point, they would recognize the family members and close friends in the audience, and that would be it.

I thought a better way to do this would be to actually tell stories and, when I could, connect some dots. I often used our American history as the way to think about that. It wasn't always military history, but I tried to bring something interesting, to give the audience something they hadn't heard before. I wanted to go beyond simply giving the chronology of the person's career—typically, the audience had a printed program in front of them and could read all that. Rather than tell them what they had probably read before the event even started, why not engage them in a different way?

I didn't really think of it as a performance, like a live play, a movie, or a television program. It wasn't about entertainment. It was about drawing people in. "Here's what you might not know. Here are some things you probably haven't heard or haven't heard in this way before. Finally, here's what that has to do with the person we're honoring."

I spent a lot of time researching, writing, refining, and preparing to tell those stories. For many years, before I went into these events, I did all my own research and writing ahead of time and asked a series of probative questions about the honorees so I could make it more personal, relatable, interesting, and informative. I learned things about them that sometimes leaders won't even think about asking. We discussed moments that matter in the last chapter; this is the same kind of thing. It was finding out what mattered to those individuals.

For example, I would say, "Tell me some things that you're most proud of in your personal or professional life." I would then add that to my comments. Quite often, these were things that very few people in the audience—maybe only close family members or friends—would even know about this person. I was bringing something new into the conversation.

To this day, even though at the time of this writing I've been retired from the Air Force for more than a year and a half, I still have people asking me to officiate ceremonies within the Department of Defense. I officiated three in the year after I retired, and a couple more are on my schedule in the coming months.

I know that at some point those requests will go away or diminish in frequency. Fortunately, in my new roles and responsibilities, I've also been asked to do public speaking and public-facing events. Whether these are live webinars on a variety of subjects or podcasts with various types and stripes, I'm doing the same kinds of things. I'm preparing in much the same way, and I go into those events really having thought through the words I'm going to use.

INSPIRATION, ASPIRATION, AND EDUCATION

In our discussion of moments that matter in chapter 7, I described the commander's calls I had the occasion to lead during my career. One thing I made an effort to do when preparing for these all-call events was to put things together so that they would connect over time. In my role

as installation commander, or city mayor, at the Air Force
Academy, for example, I was in front of the entire organization for these calls on nine different occasions. I knit all
nine of the messages together. In my last such event, before I
returned to the Pentagon for my third and final assignment
there, I shared with the entire team that, whether they knew
it or not, we had been on a very deliberately threaded-
together sequence of events during those calls. I laid out
how I'd started by introducing myself during the first call,
and then during the eight subsequent commander's calls I'd
connected each message to the themes of messages that had
come before.

Every time I'm in front of people, regardless of the
event, I want them to learn something. I think of it this way:
It's part inspiration, part aspiration, and part education. Not
every person within earshot of my voice will be inspired by
something I say, but they might hear something aspirational—a description of something they'll want to reach for. It
could be a small goal or a large one, but I want them to leave
feeling, *Yes! There is something I can do. I can get a professional
certification, further my college education, and/or connect more
closely to my teammates to accomplish a specific operational objective.* One of my main desires was to energize and encourage
people not just to think about something they might do one
day but to do something now.

Maybe they learn something of historical value or of
value to the work they're doing, like a way to take care of
the men and women they serve and support. I'm always

thinking, *Can I give them a little nugget about how to engage in this topic that maybe they hadn't thought about before?* It was really important to me to deliver at least one of those three things—inspiration, aspiration, or education—every time I was in front of people. Even to this day, if I'm speaking on a podcast or delivering a keynote, I'm looking for every member of the audience to take away one of those three things. If they come away with even one of them, that's a bonus.

None of that is possible unless I'm putting in the effort to think through the words, graphics, and videos I use during those engagements. Again, whether I'm writing them, speaking them, or both, I'm looking for the right words to connect with people.

The way to put together words that can be inspirational, aspirational, or educational is clearly through our own preparation and perspiration as leaders. Sometimes we'll have to sweat this out. It's not easy. However, the men and women with whom we're communicating deserve our dedication, devotion, and deliberateness to the process. Some may well demand it from us as their leaders, and they should. We can't try to be something we're not, like a world-famous actor (unless you *are* a world-famous actor reading this book). We don't want people to think we're just trying to perform a scripted role that's been handed to us. No, when we communicate and endeavor to choose our words wisely, we still have to be authentically ourselves. We can't adopt a new voice or persona. Rather, we should find what's vibrant and vigorous in ourselves and make that what people see.

Because if we're inauthentic, it will come through, and we won't be inspirational, aspirational, or educational at all.

For example, I try to write the way I speak. Try reading aloud what you write. If it sounds a little like a song, or if it reads like lyrics, it will probably resonate. After all, there's a reason, for example, that modern pop music "strikes a chord" with people. Take your favorite band or musician. The words that resonate with you are presumably things they thought through very deliberately. There's a reason the refrain, hook, or bridge of a song sticks in our minds for years and years—it hits us authentically where we are.

To show you what this looks like in practice, I've put together a bonus resource called "The Art of Communication." It consists of nineteen messages that I wrote to more than two thousand globally distributed team members across the entire Air Force during my last active-duty assignment prior to military retirement. You can get it for free at themissionofleadership.com/resources (or scan this QR code to be taken directly there).

Those messages transmit a lot of what we've discussed in this chapter.

In them, you'll find history and hear from famous people, many of whom you'll recognize. You'll see facts and figures. You'll also see how I tried to connect the dots across all of those messages. It's not necessarily that the nineteen messages are knitted together like one big, beautiful blanket, but you'll see as you go from one monthly message to the next how they're connected and how I tried to keep them aligned.

My direct reports and I were trying to create inspiration, aspiration, and education among our teammates, and there are two reasons that were really important (other than the reasons already given). These key things came from my boss, from the time I took the job as the director for Air Force Manpower Organization and Resources, Lieutenant General Brian Kelly (now retired). He was the chief human capital officer for the US Air Force. You could think of me at that time as one of General Kelly's deputy chief human capital officers, or CHCOs.

"Number one," he said, "I need you to make sure that there is no daylight between you, the CFO (chief financial officer), and the others who are involved in our budgeting process for the Department of the Air Force."

How would I go about doing that? Well, it was about being word wise, ensuring that I was communicating with the team I was leading, my peers, and in some cases with my superiors, in a way that would close any gaps that might come through. These gaps wouldn't have been anyone's fault; it's just a fact that sometimes, when you get into day-to-day operations, you become a little bit less tied together or tethered in the same way. We needed to make sure we sewed tight the fabric of that blanket, so to speak.

I needed to make sure I was communicating with other executives in a way that was authentic but also concise because they didn't have a lot of time. It meant resisting the idea of writing a multi-page missive or message to them, when a paragraph or a few sentences were all I really needed to make sure they understood. Sure, at times I would need to write something longer, but in those cases, I was thinking about the 1,600 men and women across the globe whom I was directly and deliberately charged with leading.

The second thing General Kelly asked me to do was to elevate the relevance of the community. One of my big responsibilities was to ensure that we properly budgeted for all the men and women in the Air Force. That way, when the president's budget was submitted to Congress and it went through the sausage-making process, we had properly accounted for all the human resources we would need at the right level of funding to execute the Air Force's mission. In short, it was my responsibility, and it was around $64 billion dollars per year—a big responsibility, to say the least.

When I started thinking about our people operating in about eighty different locations around the planet, I realized my words needed to be able to connect them because I may never be in the same room with most of them. When I did get out to do "battlefield circulation" at a couple dozen locations, I met with people in person. Again, I thought very deliberately and deeply about the things I was going to communicate to them when we got together, whether we were in a town hall or a smaller forum, such as a meal or coffee with a group.

* * *

Whether we're creating a high-level strategic document, briefing, or all-call or just chatting over coffee, we simply must be wise about every single word we use—every word we write, every word we speak—and if we make that effort, we'll become much more effective leaders.

It takes deliberate thought and focused energy. It also takes time. A good leader organizes their work so that they have time for the most important things, not the least of which is coming up with the right inspirational, aspirational, and educational words to connect with the people with whom they work. We opened this chapter with a quote: "Use your words to inspire and encourage others." This sentiment and statement also impact and influence how we use our precious daily minutes and moments. That's the subject of the next chapter.

CHAPTER 10
CLOSE FIGHT,
STRATEGIC HORIZON

He flung himself from the room, flung himself upon his
horse, and rode madly off in all directions.

—Stephen Leacock

As we climb the leadership ladder, it matters more and more how we organize our calendars to maximize our effectiveness.

When you're a young professional just getting started in your career, it's a little easier to manage your time because the demands are different. You'll have fewer resources to control or manage as a leader, from people to budgets. On the personal side, at the start of your career, you might be single or newly married, but you may not have started a family yet. Certainly, though, as you grow in your professional and personal lives, things will get more complicated.

I mean it in a good way, but it's a fact that later in our careers, we have to think more deliberately about how to harmonize our time to be most effective as leaders.

Over the course of my career, I've come across a number of different time-management models and methods. In 1974, *The Harvard Business Review* published an article by William Oncken and Donald L. Wass entitled "Management Time: Who's Got the Monkey?" This piece, which is still widely referenced more than half a century later, discussed why great leaders must prioritize keeping the number of "monkeys on their back" to a manageable minimum. The authors basically exhorted leaders not to let the people who report to them offload too many of their monkeys—projects, problems, to-dos, or things they're wrestling with—onto the leader's back. As leaders, we do sometimes need to take on some of those things for the people on our teams. However, if we take on all the monkeys our people want to put on our backs, how will we have enough minutes in the day to maximize our own leadership effectiveness?

Not Everything Is Urgent

To paraphrase Dwight D. Eisenhower, commander of the Allied forces in World War II and later president of the United States, "If everything in front of me is urgent, nothing is." The key is figuring out what is most pressing to do at any moment throughout the day. Naturally, some things take only a couple of minutes or even seconds, like a quick email in which you're just responding with "Thank you, I have this." On the other hand, when things take longer, we may not be able to take them from A to Z in one sitting. We have to be thoughtful about putting our calendars together in a way that works best for us.

There will almost always be much more that needs done than we have time for in any given day. I tend to be a bit of a perfectionist, and I write and use lists, but there are more and less effective ways to use them. In one model, you put little squares next to each item and check them off as you work through them. I'd call that a "laundry list" of things to do, but it doesn't necessarily categorize the items based on the time they take or deadlines.

Looking more critically at the list, a good leader always asks, *What's the most important thing for me to focus on here? Which items won't lead to problems if I don't get them done today or this week? Not that they don't matter at all, but which monkeys on my back don't matter as much as the others?*

CLOSE FIGHT VS. STRATEGIC HORIZON

When I arrived at US Central Command in 2007, I came across the two terms that form the title of this chapter: *close fight* and *strategic horizon*. These were category labels my boss used to categorize the things he needed to handle—the monkeys on his back.

As you can imagine, fighting an enemy that's directly on top of you is very different from fighting one you can just make out in the distance. So the close fights were the things that needed to be done right away—not long-term events or projects or programs that needed to be gradually moved along. For me, an example could be as simple as "This week I owe one of our senior leaders a policy paper updating them on a particular project." That would be high on the close fight list for that week. In a standard workweek, I would come in on Monday morning, sit down, and spend some time working these things out so I could prioritize the close fights on my schedule.

The boss would group tasks by starting with whatever was due in the next five to seven days. Those were the first priorities on the close fight list. Next, he would consider what was due in the next two to three weeks. Next, what was coming up thirty days out?

Anything due thirty days later and beyond went in the strategic horizon category. He would put all to-dos in priority order, grouped by the time horizon he thought they would take or by when the final product was due. Anything with a due date was clearly noted, so it was plain to see when time needed to be allocated to that item.

Most broadly, Monday's planning session gave a view of what was coming due in five to seven days, and each day, the lists needed to be revisited, asking, *What do I really need to get done today, and what small thing can I do to keep a long-term project moving along?*

I carried this time-management structure with me for many years. I found it was a very effective way to prioritize my own work, and it didn't take a lot of time to organize. It didn't need to include all the excruciating detail, just a few words or a single sentence for each to-do.

When you're in a close fight, it's easy to lose focus. It was always very helpful to have that document handy, and it was often just two pages—two PowerPoint charts. I used it to keep my eye on the things that were most urgent and kept referring back to it throughout the workweek to make sure I stayed on time and target.

The strategic horizon is about organizing things by due date and thinking through them more longitudinally. That doesn't mean we don't chip away at things that have a due date six months from now. It just recognizes we don't need to try to finish the whole thing now because we have other competing priorities. Day-to-day things will pop up and need our attention—what we sometimes refer to as "the fires that flare."

In general, this framework made it easier to organize my own calendar. I routinely used those two pages to "code" my calendar in whatever way would be helpful. Some items were coded as administrative work. Some were coded as writing time or project preparation—whatever would remind me to deliberately put aside time for something I couldn't finish in a day or a week.

When writing my monthly messages to my team, for example, as I described in the "Word Wise" chapter, I had to deliberately put time on my calendar to develop and write them. (You can read nineteen of these monthly messages in The Art of Communication bonus resource. Get it for free by visiting themissionofleadership.com/resources, or scan this QR code.)

Those missives would start off on the strategic horizon chart because I wanted to publish them on the first Wednesday of every month.

To consistently make that deadline, I needed to schedule time to work on them as the month went along. In time, people came to know that the first Wednesday of each month, they would see that message in their inbox from the boss.

As all strategic horizon items moved within the thirty-day mark, they became close fight items. When writing those monthly messages, I found my organizational system helpful in that I had constant reminders: Now it's two weeks out. Now it's a week out. Now it's Monday before I'm going to send it, and I need to make sure I've actually done the work. All I was really doing was going back constantly and refining my two charts. Doing things in this way made it easier for me to organize my calendar. I had conditioned myself to focus on the things that mattered most.

It also made it easier to communicate with my boss consistently. My bosses, across the arc of my career from 2007 until my retirement in 2023, all knew that I had organized things in a very specific way, though I naturally made some adjustments to align to each of their communication styles. By and large, though, I maintained the basic framework of the close fight and strategic horizon across those sixteen years.

WHATEVER YOUR SYSTEM, MAKE IT WORK FOR YOU

My system also helped me schedule things early so I could get them done with the quality that I wanted. For example, I know myself well enough to know that first thing in the morning was not the best time for writing. I'm not a morning person. I tend to get going much more around noon, and that's when my mind is working best. With that in mind, I could schedule tasks during the time of day when I'd be most productive for each one. Also, the end of the business day (or "duty day," as we say in the military) was probably not the time for me to get deep in thought. Sometimes that happened anyway because of late-breaking things that needed my attention. Whenever I could be, though, I was deliberate about organizing my calendar to account for the ebb and flow of my own highest-level productivity.

Returning to the smile-producing Stephen Leacock quote at the beginning of the chapter, what happens to leaders if we don't take time to think through what's close versus what's more strategic in nature? We may well "ride madly off in all directions" instead of knowing exactly where our attention is needed day to day, month to month, and year over year. Good leaders use a time-management system that works for them, that helps them work through their day with focus and purpose to inform, inspire, and lead their teams.

MAKE YOUR BED

One good idea, according to behavioral science, is to put a few easy tasks on your calendar every day. You can knock those out first thing in the morning, which was often my practice. I cleared and responded to messages—emails, texts, and voicemails. I read and responded to posts people sent me on LinkedIn. If I found things that I needed to return to later because they needed a longer or more thoughtful response, or if I needed to do some work before I sent the response, I would just flag them in my email inbox to revisit later in my day. At any rate, there were a few things I knew I could take care of first thing, and that way I accomplished something every single day.

I think sometimes we fail to acknowledge or under-stand that responding to email or messages is actual work. Typically, it's far-and-away more than answering or addressing a bunch of flip comments that you don't really need to think about, and people are usually waiting for your response. I tried desperately to respond to every message I received within twenty-four hours. It's a pet peeve of mine. If I sent a message to somebody and I needed a response, but days went by without one, I'd begin to wonder if they even received it. What then? Do you find yourself resending the message? Sometimes you need to do that to remind the person on the other end, who might have become overwhelmed with the monkeys on their own back. I deliberately established a good practice of being responsive. If a message needed a longer response and I knew I probably couldn't fully respond on that same workday or as a close fight, I at least acknowledged I had received it and would come back with periodic updates. Even if you don't see clearing your messages as work, you can think of it as just picking some low-hanging fruit at the start of the day. That way, you always have something you've completed that day, and you've started to build momentum for the rest of your close fights.

There's a great book by Admiral William H. McRaven entitled *Make Your Bed: Little Things That Can Change Your Life and Maybe the World*. Admiral McRaven is a retired four-star Admiral and Navy SEAL who led Special Operations Command for the United States military, and he used the premise of his book in the commencement address he delivered at the University of Texas at Austin in 2014. His simple idea was this: Every day, when you get up, take a couple of minutes to make your bed. That way, no matter what happens throughout the day, whether your entire schedule comes apart or you're consumed by some urgent matter that comes up, when you get to the end of the day and you're ready to go to sleep, you'll be reminded that at least one thing got accomplished that day. I love that imagery. It shows the importance of finding a couple of easy things to do to start your day, because doing so builds momentum and gives you a little confidence (even courage, in some cases) to carry on.

Some days are going to be wonderful and easy, but others will be challenging and difficult for any leader. On those tough days, knowing that we always have a few small things accomplished will keep us on track.

YOU DON'T HAVE TO TAKE ON EVERY MONKEY

It's also important to recognize that when we're managing our time as leaders, we can't say no to everything, but a strong leader doesn't say yes to everything either. I learned this lesson many, many times. I'm still learning it! We're all human, we don't want to disappoint people, and we want people to continue asking us for help because it makes us feel appreciated (or even admired). I'm no exception. I've had to guard my back against the overpopulation of monkeys. I need to remind myself to be thoughtful about not automatically saying yes to everything.

Earlier in my professional life, I was a "yes to everything" person. That very quickly led to being overwhelmed because I hadn't thought more judiciously about the time I have during any given day, week, or month. I just tried to be a people pleaser. That doesn't work, and it doesn't make you an effective leader.

Now, while I still tend to say yes more than no, I'm also still purposeful about choosing *when* I say yes or no. This makes it easier to keep from overwhelming either my close fight or strategic horizon list.

As leaders, we need to model these choices for our people. When we are asked to tackle something, or we're given a project or a product to deliver to the market, we want to make sure we're delivering something we can be proud of. It doesn't matter whether we're just writing a document or helping the innovators and creators in an organization satisfy a client. As leaders, we should be proud of every single thing we provide. At the same time, we also need to be good teammates, carrying out our share of the work.

A Harmonized Life Requires Good Time Management

Every leader I've admired has had a good handle on their own calendar, understood their own limitations, and accounted for those limitations in their routines. For example, there's General Kelly, whom I talked about in the previous chapters and with whom I'm still connected to this day. One of the many, many things I admired about him is that he modeled some really important things to all the men and women on his team. When I worked for him, he had an enormous amount of pressure and responsibility on his shoulders, for sure. One thing he was very consistent about, though, was that he was gone from the office by 5:30 or 6 p.m. Unless something popped up and he just couldn't leave, he left the office in time to go home and have dinner with his wife.

Now, he might get back online, and often he was back on his email and checking messages and doing work after he had dinner, but he found ways to properly prioritize (or "harmonize," as suggested earlier) that personal part of his life.

As I've shared, this is something I didn't do particularly well during the whole of my career. Over and over again, there were times I could have been better at harmonizing my work and personal time. I could have been more mindful. Once in a while, my wife would call and remind me that I had a family and it was okay to come home. I say that with tongue in cheek, but I did need to remind myself I had other obligations to be thoughtful about.

As we covered in earlier chapters, I think the notion of "work-life balance" is a fallacy. It's like chasing the pot of gold at the end of the rainbow—it doesn't really exist. I think harmonizing the different parts of your life is a much better way to think about it. For example, if you finish early on a given day, you could dig into some of those strategic horizon to-dos, but it might be better harmony to spend that precious time with your family.

A good leader is thoughtful about those things and incorporates them into their planning. When I was sharing my close fight and strategic horizon charts with my bosses, all the personal things were not on there, but they were surely on my calendar so that I could attend to them. I missed more of those personal events than I should have, but I learned later that I needed to set better parameters for myself.

Deeply encouraged by my wife, we created what I call "between the sevens." What I meant by this, which I shared with my last three bosses in the Air Force and Space Force before I retired, was that I deliberately planned to operate between 7 a.m. and 7 p.m. I wouldn't be reading messages, responding to things, or doing any actual work before 7 a.m. or after 7 p.m., and my bosses respected that.

As with any rule, there will always be exceptions. At times, things would happen that required a leader to be in earlier, stay later, or both, and that's okay. As leaders, we need to communicate such parameters to the people we work with so that they know what to expect from us. I didn't just tell the people I worked for about my rule; I also communicated it to my entire team. People understood that if they sent me something at 8 p.m. or 6 a.m., I wouldn't respond immediately. If something outside the sevens needed my urgent attention, they needed to call me. "I'll pick up my cell phone, and I'll answer it when I see that it's you," I would say. For the most part, though, I deliberately disciplined myself to operate only between the sevens.

My teammates could be comforted knowing that the reverse would also apply—they wouldn't see things coming to them from me at 9 or 10 p.m. Most email systems include a function that enables you to delay when a message is sent, so if I had a late-night brainstorm that needed to be expressed in an email, I became accustomed to using the

"Schedule Send" function or just kept it in draft form to ensure it didn't get sent outside the sevens.

This matters. If you communicate this kind of parameter to your team, but you don't model it consistently, it will be very easy to confuse your people. I had a teammate who was most productive after midnight, and it worked for them. I often reminded them not to send emails at 1 or 2 a.m., particularly to people that worked for them, even if they included the disclaimer "I don't need you to respond until your normal working hours." What happens if you send that email in the middle of the night anyway, even with the disclaimer? It's not hard science, but my experience was that only about one-third of the people we tell not to respond in the middle of the night will believe what we say. Another third won't believe us, thinking it's a test, and these people will actually set their electronic devices to alert them when something comes in from us at any hour. They'll get out of bed and try to respond as quickly as possible, within minutes, to "pass" the test. The other third will be confused about whether to respond, having received a very mixed message from us.

* * *

Consistency equals clarity. When we manage our close fights and strategic horizons in a disciplined, deliberate, clear, and consistent way; communicate our operating parameters to the people we work with; and stick to our guidelines as consistently as possible, good things happen.

We'll find we've increased the degree to which people will connect, collaborate, and communicate with us.

Being consistent means doing what you say you're going to do, without fail. Good leaders have strong discipline in their professional time management, and they're consistent.

That doesn't mean, however, that great leaders never fail. Let's dive deeply into understanding that failure is not defeat.

PART III
FAILURE IS NOT DEFEAT

Success is not final,
failure is not fatal.
It is the courage to continue that counts.
—Winston Churchill

CHAPTER 11
FAIL FALLING FORWARD

I never fail. I either win or learn.

—Nelson Mandela

I love this quote from Nelson Mandela. The truth of the matter is that every leader is going to fail. No one bats 1.000. It's not truly possible.

That doesn't mean we shouldn't always strive to do well, but sometimes things aren't going to work the way we intend them to. In fact, sometimes we'll have a failure or fracture that is really deep and could even be destructive and debilitating to an organization. I'm not suggesting we intend to fail, but it's likely to happen anyway. The more teams we lead, the more we increase the likelihood of some failure along the way, large or small. Failures are characterized by what I often refer to as missteps, miscues, or mistakes.

It's not about whether we *will* fail during our careers as leaders. It's about how we'll respond when we do. What do we do with failure? Borrowing again from Mandela, when we fail, we should learn something from it.

That's really critical. When we fail, we should ask ourselves, *What am I learning from this experience? How can I try to avoid this in the future?* Then, as we recover and repair or restore the failure, *How can this make me a better leader? How does this lesson improve the way my teammates operate? How does it make the organization even better?*

Across the arc of my career, I have failed many more times than I remember or care to remember. I learned very early in my career that, despite my best intentions, I was going to make mistakes. Let me share a couple of ways I failed and what I learned from those experiences.

OWNING MY FIRST $25,000 MISTAKE

When I was a brand-new second lieutenant in the US Air Force, I made a $25,000 mistake. Specifically, I used the wrong type of resource to make a purchase—like paying for something out of the wrong account.

In the US government, there are different "colors of money," which is like having different accounts for different purposes. We have appropriated funds, which are the dollars that Congress authorizes and then appropriates for specific purposes. These are taxpayer dollars. There are also non-appropriated funds, which do not come from the taxpayer. At every US military installation, there are for-profit businesses. Many of those receive some taxpayer funding to support their operations, but others don't. Just like any other business, they have to make a profit to stay in operation.

At the time, I happened to be leading one of the organizations that needed to make a profit to remain fully operable despite receiving some taxpayer funding support. I was very young and very new, so I didn't realize that there were different funding sources for different purposes. I made a necessary procurement that cost $25,000 for my chief logistician, who had come to me and indicated he needed some supplies. I went to our accountant and asked, "What's our cash flow situation look like? What do we have in accounts receivable and accounts payable? I need to make a smart decision about whether we can afford this $25,000 purchase."

Everything looked good on the balance sheet and on our profit-and-loss (P&L) statement. I thought we were in a good spot, so I gave the logistician the authority to make the purchase. As it turned out, he was supposed to use appropriated taxpayer dollars, not non-appropriated dollars. That's how I learned that there were different funding sources to manage. Another leader in the organization—akin to a CFO—called me and said, "I think you've made a procurement mistake. Please come talk to me about it." She was right. In military terminology, I used the wrong resource type.

At that time, this $25,000 error was not a small mistake. I asked the CFO for advice. "It's difficult," she said, "but I know we can fix this. There are mechanisms for righting this wrong, recouping those dollars that were incorrectly applied, and then correctly applying the right kind of dollars."

Besides the lesson that I was going to make mistakes on occasion, this episode also taught me to do something I tried to carry out from that point forward: Ask more questions. I got better at asking more questions before a decision was made, but in some cases, still more questions needed to be asked.

When I was confronted with this situation at the outset of my career, I resisted the temptation some leaders may feel to pass the buck. I didn't say, "Well, nobody told me!" I learned it doesn't really matter whether that was true. In this case it was true, but that would be a simple deflection. Leaders don't deflect. They understand that whether they direct the mistake themselves or it occurs downline within the organization, ultimately they're still responsible.

I owned it. I learned what we needed to do to fix it. I learned from the situation, and my team learned from it. Instead of saying to my accountant, "You steered me wrong," or to my logistician, "You should have known better—you've been in this role for years," I owned that we had made a mistake and said, "Let's learn from this. Let's make sure we don't do this again."

Ultimately, in my career as a leader, I knew I was going to make new and different mistakes along the way.

TRUST, BUT VERIFY: ANOTHER $25,000 MISTAKE

Later in my career, my team made another mistake valued at around $25,000. (Don't think I only make mistakes $25,000 at a time—it's just a coincidence.)

We had contracted an organization to credential men and women working in our base fitness centers to become certified personal trainers. This was very important for us because, as we describe it, these people were "maintaining the human weapon system." We wanted our teammates to understand anatomy, physiology, and kinesiology, so we contracted with an organization to deliver that training. When our teammates passed their exams at the end of the training, they would become certified trainers.

The first part of the course lasted five days, and the second part three days. About halfway through, it was brought to my attention that we hadn't actually paid the company that was conducting the training. The trainers on-site asked when their remittance was going to come because we had a responsibility to pay them up front, not at the end of delivery. I was a little shocked to learn we hadn't paid the bill ahead of time, and if challenged, this could be a violation of federal law. We might have had a real legal issue here.

I hadn't gone back to check whether the financial manager had paid the contractor before their personnel arrived on base to train and certify our fifty-some teammates. Again, I could have passed the buck. I could have told the financial manager I knew I'd given clear directions to pay the contractor weeks in advance. As we researched where things went wrong, it did appear as though our communication, via email, had become somewhat blurred.

What I learned from this mistake was to heed the old Russian proverb popularized by President Ronald Reagan: "Trust, but verify." Reagan used the phrase with regard to nuclear proliferation and of course, I hadn't made a nuclear mistake. But as the leader, it was incumbent upon me to verify that the contractor was paid before the service was rendered.

Instead of blaming the financial manager, just like we did with the first $25,000 mistake, we tried to make it a learning experience and fix the problem. I learned, or relearned, that when we're in leadership, we need to trust, but verify. There are times we need to make sure we proverbially cross the T's and dot the I's. By extension, this was an opportunity for the entire team to learn. The lesson was that when we're involved with contractual arrangements, we must undertake the due diligence to make sure everything is where it needs to be.

Don't Make a Bad Situation Worse

Without a doubt, the biggest failure in my entire Air Force career occurred when I was at the Air Force Academy.

Federal law requires all federal agencies and departments to have inspectors general (IGs), who examine policies, processes, and procedures to make sure not only that the organization is following the law but that it's also maintaining good ethics and sound operating principles. This is an important part of demonstrating that we are, in fact, capable of doing the things the public we serve has charged us to do. The Academy had a three-year inspection cycle—a thirty-six-month, end-to-end inspection regimen.

At the end of the three years, we had a capstone unit effectiveness inspection. This meant about eighty people descended upon the Academy to make sure my team, the Tenth Airbase Wing, or Team Ten, as I called them (charged with servicing and supporting the physical installation and all the cadets, faculty, and assigned personnel), was fulfilling our mission in the most effective way possible.

I assumed command of the unit about eight months before that capstone event, which meant more than two-thirds of the inspection cycle had already passed. I recognized there were some things we hadn't done particularly well. Nevertheless, sixty days into a new position, the new commander is required to give their boss a unit "health report" detailing how they think the unit is doing. As part of the current inspection regimen, there were three things I highlighted that I thought needed to be improved. It turned out that when we failed that capstone inspection eight months later, I was proven prescient about those things.

That's not to say I handled everything well, because I didn't. If I were really, really good, I would've realized the depth of the challenges we had, but I didn't. In this regard, I leaned a little too much on simply trusting my teammates without requiring enough accountability. That's on me as the leader, not on anybody in my IG office or anywhere else around the three-thousand-person organization. It was my responsibility to dig deeper, but just as I had as a brand-new second lieutenant giving permission for an erroneous $25,000 purchase, I needed to ask more questions than I did.

The capstone is typically a five-day on-site evaluation. I knew by Wednesday, midway through the week and review, that we were highly unlikely to pass that inspection. The evaluation included four components, and we were going to pass three, but on "improving the unit," we were going to fail. If we failed that component, we failed the entire inspection. We simply weren't looking closely enough at the things that weren't going well inside the unit and appropriately addressing them.

At the end of the capstone inspection on Friday, the IG team lead came to me and my leadership team and confirmed we had failed the inspection. At the end of that late afternoon meeting, I dismissed the rest of my team. I told them to go home and prepare for what would happen the following week while I communicated the news to my boss.

I got in my car and drove the seven and a half miles from my office to my boss's office on the Air Force Academy grounds. That was an interesting trip. For those who don't know, from my office at the south end of the Academy to my boss's office on the college campus proper, there was about a 1,200-foot rise in elevation. As I drove up the hill, the temperature dropped. The April sky turned from blue to gray, and it started snowing. That did match my mood—what had started as a bright, beautiful day had gone dark. I don't know if that would be considered poetic justice, or maybe just a coincidence, but the weather matched how I felt.

When I arrived at my boss's office, I knew he was off the installation on a business trip. I got ahold of his deputy and told him what had happened. The two of us went into the boss's office and called him with the news. I won't forget his reply.

"You have until Monday."

He paused after that, and I thought he was giving me until Monday to clear out my office. I was a wing commander, usually the most senior command position people will ever hold in the Air Force since only about one in a hundred colonels become generals. A major failure at this level often meant the end of the line. Since I'd failed at that apex, it would've been within my boss's authority to ask me to pack up my office.

That's not actually what he said, though. Including the pause, he said, "You have until Monday . . . to get over it, because I need you to lead that wing back. They'll need you more than ever before."

It turned out he paused because we had caught him in the middle of an exercise run, and he was simply catching his breath. The pause had a dramatic effect I don't think the boss intended. But I was thinking I really had failed in an unrecoverable way this time.

As a three-star general and a former IG himself, he had seen a few of these things before. But as a colonel, I hadn't. The general continued, "Look, you need to take the weekend, these next 48 hours or so, to get yourself right. You need to be clear about what happened here and how to communicate it to your team."

As I mentioned earlier, typically when I address the team verbally, I don't use notes. The general knew that, and he cautioned me. "You need to make sure you write down and read to the team every single word, and you need to be very, very thoughtful about those words. They need to be entered into the official record."

He was exactly right. I took the weekend to "get myself right." I spent somewhere between sixteen and twenty hours over those next two days to get clear about what I knew, what we needed to do next, and where we needed to put our effort and energy, and then to write my message. Monday morning, I called my entire senior leadership team, in this case about thirty people, into my conference room. I read the four-page document I'd carefully considered and created, verbatim, and then shared that same document with them electronically. Not only did they hear what I said but they also had the opportunity to revisit those words as many times as necessary.

I learned another difficult lesson. I discovered that I could fix this mistake, just like the other mistakes I had made earlier in my career, though it would be a long and tough process to make things right. I learned that even as a senior leader, you're still going to make mistakes.

Leadership is easy when things are going well. It's very easy to sail smoothly when the water is like glass, the wind is blowing, and there's nothing obstructing you. It's really hard, though, when you hit choppy waters. I've often said that in moments of difficulty, sometimes even in moments of danger, true character is revealed. Who are you when these things happen? Who are you when they happen again? Do you own your mistakes, or do you play the blame game?

Do you recognize when and where you need help?

No Leader Is Alone

It would be easy, particularly as senior leaders, to assume we know what needs to happen next. In the case of the failed inspection at the Academy, though, making such an assumption would've been a fool's errand. If I had understood the depth of the challenge, we wouldn't have failed in the first place. That was another big lesson for me: As I continued to climb the leadership ladder, I needed to be more probative, more inquisitive, more involved. Not that I didn't trust people or wasn't giving them the authority to make decisions, but I needed to be asking the right kinds of questions and keep asking until I was fully satisfied that a way forward had emerged.

I also learned that it's really important for a leader to get the sequencing right and to know when to share bad news, not because I wasn't going to be transparent or authentic but because I needed to understand the landscape.

Recall that I sat down with the senior leadership team, around thirty people, on Monday morning and shared the news with them. At the end of that session, I directed them not to tell anyone in their organization or in their business units what the results were. It was my responsibility and role as the seniormost leader to deliver the inspection results.

I planned to give the bad news to the entire three-thousand-person organization on Friday morning, four days later. The reason I wanted to wait until Friday morning was that on Thursday afternoon, we were holding our quarterly awards ceremony. You can imagine that if I had done it before the ceremony highlighting the best and brightest from the previous quarter, many of whom were being rewarded for the great work they had done to prepare for the very inspection we failed (not their fault!), it would have turned a happy event into a very somber one. It's definitely not the environment you want for that type of event. For that reason, I deliberately delayed the announcement of the bad news. It was important for us to be together Thursday afternoon to celebrate the goodness of the things we had done right and well the previous quarter, highlight people for the great things they had done individually, and congratulate the teams that won awards.

When Friday morning came, I didn't want to give the team a sourness as we headed into that weekend, but just to plainly inform them. "As a matter of fact," I said, "this is mostly my fault. I'm going to own this failure, but I need you, my teammates, to help me get this fixed." I then laid out the framework for how we were going to fix it.

Four months later, we passed a full reevaluation with flying colors. Some really interesting things happened as a result of this experience. Not only did we learn a number of things, but as the outgrowth of that failure, we put into play best practices that other units and teams around the Air Force had adopted for themselves and their organizations. I know so, because for a couple of years after that series of events, other senior leaders came to me and told me they were using some of the processes, policies, and products that Team Ten had put together in response to this failure. We created new operating principles to make sure we got it right, that we were wholly mission effective, and that we would be so perpetually.

* * *

First Lieutenant Clebe McClary, United States Marine Corps, is a true American hero. Clebe was badly injured in Vietnam. He lost an eye and an arm and sustained shrapnel damage all over his body, which led to his medical retirement when he came back to the States.

When I was a young captain, a young professional, Clebe came to speak to my class at Squadron Officer School, a first-level leadership training and development program all Air Force captains and officers are required to complete, usually four to six years into their careers. Talk about "word wise"—his remarks were definitely inspirational, aspirational, and educational. His central message was his concept of FIDO: "Forget It and Drive On."

Clebe didn't mean we should forget our failures by pretending they had never happened. He meant we shouldn't let one failure lead to another by dwelling on it.

This lesson was driven home to me many times over my career. Fail falling forward. Reveal your great leadership character by the way you respond to failure. Forget it and drive on. When you don't win, learn.

CHAPTER 12
POOPY DIAPERS

Few things can help an individual
more than to place responsibility on him and
to let him know that you trust him.

—Booker T. Washington

Think about a kid in preschool who poops in their pants. The smell is blamed on everyone.

What I'm getting at here is that, over the arc of my career, it has occurred to me how many times we made everyone in the organization pay for the mistakes or failures of one person or one team within the larger organization. As a leader, halfway through my military career, I recognized this is wrong. When something happens, you should go to the source of the challenge, concern, or mistake. You can use it as a learning example to teach others to avoid similar mistakes, but be very careful about holding the entire organization or a broader team accountable for the mistakes of the few or the single person.

One example comes from years ago, when I was assigned to US Central Command—the command that's responsible for the Middle East, northern Africa, and central Asia. At the time I was there, 2007–2010, our nation was at the height of Operation Enduring Freedom in Afghanistan and Operation Iraqi Freedom in Iraq. As you can appreciate, with everything going on during that time, we were moving at the speed of light organizationally and to a person. Hundreds of thousands of men and women were engaged in these efforts, and sometimes mistakes would be made. I'm not talking about catastrophic mistakes that could lead to the worst possible outcomes for whichever human was engaged in those efforts; I just mean that sometimes we made policy mistakes, procedural mistakes, or process mistakes.

I'm recalling a day at the command headquarters in Tampa, Florida. There were several thousand people working there at the time, and one person mistakenly inserted a classified thumb drive into an unclassified computer system.

The mistake was very quickly caught, and it didn't lead to a security breach or potentially more problematic situation. It was an honest human mistake and not a terribly difficult one to make. At my workstation at Central Command, I had three completely different computer systems, and all of them had thumb drive ports. It was foreseeable that somebody might insert a device in the wrong system.

I won't fault the command leaders at the time for the way they handled the situation; I wasn't a senior leader then, and they may have had a good reason for their decision. Their reaction and decision was that, from that point forward, no one would be allowed to use a thumb drive anywhere in the organization. Up to that time, thumb drives had given us a way to transfer files very quickly between computers and between people. For example, if I was working on a decision brief or a presentation, I might just download it to a thumb drive and then take it into the conference room and put it into the computer there so it could be projected onto a large screen very quickly. We weren't using the cloud at the time, but the same could apply today—if your presentation is backed up on a thumb drive, you can bring it into the conference room quickly if the internet is down and you can't access the cloud at the moment.

It was common to back up information on thumb drives, which replaced the old floppy disk. I remember early in my career using a 3½-inch floppy disk to transfer files from place to place (and even those disks were a technological improvement over the original 5¼-inch disks).

The decision could've been different. "Let's employ better computer hygiene," they could have said, "make sure we're taking care of each individual thumb drive and being very cautious about putting the wrong thumb drive in the wrong device." Or even, "No thumb drives will be used in any of our classified systems, but they're still authorized in unclassified systems." Instead, all thumb drives were banned in the organization.

I heard one of the people I worked with use the analogy of the poopy diaper: "Now that one person here pooped their pants, we're all going to have to wear diapers."

I don't mean to be crass, but the analogy is certainly memorable (though pretty stark). One person made a mistake. It might have been a little messy, but it wasn't something serious. After all, we could have rendered the ports inoperable on classified computers through a simple software upload or at least created an authentication process to ensure that mistake would not be replicated, but nothing like that happened. We didn't need to make everybody in the organization do the penance or pay the price for one person's mistake. Rather, again, we could have used it as a teaching tool: Tell people it happened and instruct them to double their efforts to be thoughtful about their use of thumb drives.

This official reaction, though, seemed a bit emotional. It really wasn't all that different from the reaction people have if they're upset or angry or their emotions are particularly high due to an email they received. Best practice is not to simply fire back the first thing we think. It's better to write a response and then sit on the email without sending it. Maybe we come back a few hours later or the next day and think better of hitting "Send."

I've done this many times. If we aren't fully in charge of our faculties because we have an emotional response to something that smacks us and we want to respond immediately, it's better to wait. Give it a ten count or maybe a count of a couple hours. Let's not allow our first instinct to become a reaction the entire organization has to live with.

Again, this wasn't something catastrophic. By contrast, what about failing a huge product launch? The launch of "New Coke" by the Coca-Cola Company back in the mid-eighties is now a widely used case study because that launch, in retrospect and review, is seen as an enormous error. Coca-Cola covers it on their own website: "The Coca-Cola Company took arguably the biggest risk in consumer goods history, announcing that it was changing the formula for the world's most popular soft drink, and spawning consumer angst the likes of which no business has ever seen." New Coke lasted a mere seventy-nine days on the market and cost the company $30 million at the time, which is $89 million in 2025 dollars, adjusted for inflation. Ultimately, the free publicity from having such wide media coverage led to a market share increase over rival Pepsi. However, this was an unforced error despite nearly two hundred thousand taste tests that found customers would enjoy the new version.

More thought could've been employed before that launch, particularly understanding the depth and breadth of brand loyalty and consumer identification built over the prior ninety-nine years. When I talk about dealing well with failure, I'm not talking about that level of impact per se, but something at a lower level. Be thoughtful about it, and don't create the poopy diaper syndrome.

Another example predates my time at Central Command. I was in my first real leadership laboratory in the Air Force as a squadron commander, equivalent to a mid-level manager. I remember one particular Status of Discipline meeting, which was a monthly meeting. As the name implies, we were reviewing various things that had happened with our military and civilian members that were improper, sometimes unethical, and other times actually illegal.

A prime example was someone receiving a citation for driving under the influence of alcohol or drugs (DUI). When that happened, the responsible leader—the person under whom the DUI recipient worked—had to appear before the entire leadership body, usually a couple to a several dozen people, and explain what had happened. The purpose of this requirement was that we would all learn from the situation and try to prevent it from happening again, and also to ensure each leader was applying punishments, whether administrative or legal, in a fair and appropriate manner.

My thinking was that the person who committed the crime was responsible, but a senior leader charged and challenged us all to declare it a leadership issue—to believe it had happened because of a failure of leadership.

I was the most junior leader in the room, and I objected to this. I should point out that the senior leader became a great mentor of mine and still is to this day. Out of respect, I was trying not to oppose him, but I objected to the idea that I was responsible for this person making this mistake. Here's the rationale I used, which I thought was very collegial, very collaborative, and not confrontational: "Every single leader in this room has routinely, repeatedly told members of our teams—an entire team of six hundred, in my case—that if they're out drinking and need a ride home, they should use their Get Out of Jail Free card."

This incident occurred in the days before Uber and Lyft, but we did have the cooperation of all the local taxi companies. We issued cards that a person could present to a cab driver for a free ride home. There was never a need to make a mistake by getting behind the wheel of a car after drinking, whether they had one drink or way too many.

As if that weren't enough, many leaders in the organization told their teams the same thing I told mine: "Call me. I will come to get you anywhere, anytime, any place, without question, and make sure you get home safely so you don't make that misstep or mistake." There was no judgment for going out and having a good time at a club, a bar, or a restaurant with friends.

The point I was making at the Status of Discipline meeting was that every single person in that room wasn't the reason this person made this bad decision. We did not all mess up. This person had the agency to make their own decisions, even poor ones. To return to our stark analogy, that person pooped, and now we all had to wear diapers instead of addressing the single event and the single person who had made a mistake. It was my way of saying, as a leader, you have to grow, you have to go, and you have to give grace.

We grow as leaders when we become more thoughtful about how we address a bad situation inside our organization. We go forward by focusing on the thing that happened and using it as a teaching moment, not punishing everybody in the organization for the mistake of a single person or one small team (whether or not that was our intent). We have to give of our time as leaders, making the effort to have that conversation, to explain what's going on and how the organization will move forward in a better direction as a result of the incident. Finally, a good leader gives grace to people. Forgiveness is a truly powerful thing. As an organization, and more importantly as a leader, it's not about simply papering over something that might be illegal, unethical, or immoral. It's about recognizing we're human, forgiving, and allowing the opportunity to correct the error and move on.

* * *

We've already explored many of the mistakes I've made across my career. Each one taught me the importance of giving grace to others and to myself so we might all have the opportunity to learn and recover from mistakes, missteps, or miscues. This makes for better professionals and better organizations. Trust matters mightily following mistakes. People need to have ways to both recover and restore trust from us as leaders. Certainly there are situations and scenarios when that's not possible, but those are the most egregious of events. Most mistakes don't rise anywhere near that threshold.

One person makes a boo-boo. Not everybody needs to wear a diaper.

CHAPTER 13
DUNKING DUCKS

The truth is not always the same as the
majority decision.

—Pope John Paul II

Very early in my career—in fact, while I was still in my senior year of college—I started to work through *The Team Handbook*. This textbook by Barbara J. Streibel, Brian J. Joiner, and Peter R. Scholtes has been in wide use since its first publication in 1988 and is generally regarded as one of the best business books of all time. Its central aim is to provide models for forming, managing, and leading teams.

One of the models in the book is a famous framework developed by Bruce Tuckman, an American psychologist who described the five stages every team goes through:

1. Forming: choosing people to work on the team

1. Storming: jostling over various aspects of the team's work
2. Norming: gaining agreement on those aspects
3. Performing: doing the actual work
4. Adjourning: concluding the project

The book goes on to describe in detail many of a team leader's functions, from leading an effective team meeting to assigning effective roles to team members to being more effective at decision-making.

The authors also introduce great tools for team leaders. One is the Ishikawa diagram developed by a Japanese professor named Kaoru Ishikawa in the 1960s. Also known as a fishbone diagram or boat chart, the Ishikawa diagram helps a leader lay out a timeline of events that may have led to some team outcome, such as a faulty decision or mistaken action. Picture a series of right-facing arrows, each one populated by text describing a discussion, assumption, decision, or other component of a team's work that led to the next component. This is a great tool for assessing cause and effect.

Statistical analysis, applied analytical work, regression analysis—the "Bible for teams," *The Team Handbook,* covers nearly everything a new leader needs to know to be effective. One of the key things I remember from reading that book all those years ago was the danger of groupthink.

GROUPTHINK

My own way of defining groupthink is that it's a phenomenon by which every person on a team aligns with a decision without real, deliberate discussion or discourse, and it tends or trends toward the wrong decision. Unfortunately, I can't calculate how many times I saw groupthink in action during my leadership career.

Years ago, I heard an old Air Force adage: When a person takes a leadership position, they immediately become 25 percent funnier, 40 percent better-looking, and 50 percent smarter. Funny as that is, too often we tell ourselves that's pretty much what happens when we're promoted. It isn't, of course, but there is some idea that a leader is looking for people to simply agree with them rather than challenging them or others in the room in a positive way.

I'm not suggesting the conference room or decision table should devolve into fisticuffs. Rather, it's about seeking better decisions through insightful inquiry: "Are we really asking probative and purposeful questions? Are we thinking there might be a better answer to whatever we're wrestling with, or whatever decision needs to be made? Are we adequately guarding against great man or great woman syndrome—the belief that it's all about our leader having all the right information and making all the best decisions?"

A historical thought pattern suggests there's always a great person who ascends to the leadership position. I'm not arguing that there aren't great leaders from history. Some of my favorites, like Winston Churchill and, going back further, George Washington or Abraham Lincoln, were truly great leaders. Each was surrounded by an even greater team.

To take one example, the more I've read about and studied and analyzed Abraham Lincoln and his applied leadership style, the more I understand the importance he placed on having a council of rivals. He chose rivals as his advisors and even appointed rivals to his cabinet when he was president, deliberately because he wanted to avoid groupthink, generations before the term was coined. (As an aside, I think Lincoln himself was coined on the penny [ca. 1909] before the term *groupthink* was.)

Think about how an executive, or a leader at any level, would follow Lincoln's example to ensure better teamwork and decision-making. They'll seek rivals for their teams by asking who the deliberate dissenters are in the organization, or, as I prefer to think of them, the "considered contrarians." They'll look for the people who, during those discussions and deliberations, ask questions and really press in—not to be a nuisance or be noisy but to truly probe whether we are thinking about decisions as deeply as we should. They'll find the people who ask whether we're bringing enough data into a decision and whether we've asked all the right questions or posited some counter-theories.

I think about one of the leaders I worked with while we were building the Space Force. I loved the fact that he was a considered contrarian. It just so happened I didn't have to ask him to assume that role—it was naturally who he was. And it was wonderful. It was beautiful because he made our decisions much sharper. He helped us avoid getting into groupthink simply because I or some other leader came into the room with a preconceived notion of what the decision should be before we even discussed it. Having someone like him in the room made us better and more thoughtful. It made us think through different scenarios and situations to make better decisions.

This considered contrarian helped me more than once to overcome, as the senior executive in the room, my own great man syndrome. Because of his input and inquiry, we sometimes modified our decisions, and we were better for it.

DID MY RANK FALL OFF?

Years ago, one of my longtime Air Force colleagues was in a meeting with a full-bird colonel. As the discussion about a certain decision continued, the people in the room thought they were contributing, asking good questions, and being insightful or inquisitive. The colonel didn't like the direction the conversation was taking, and at one point he stopped the discussion and said, "Did my rank fall off? I'm in charge here."

Unsurprisingly, the effect of that intervention was to totally shut down the discussion. There was no more discourse about the particulars of the decision. What did the Colonel just teach everybody in the room? That they didn't have a right or reason to contribute to decisions.

This leads to what I've described in the title of the chapter: "dunking ducks." Everyone sitting around that table suddenly felt the need to dunk their heads like ducks do in a pond when they're looking for fish to eat. So much for contributing or even thinking. They decide to just feed, to just be a part of the collective and try not to ruffle anyone's feathers. (Appropriate, since we're talking about ducks.)

That was an example of a leader literally inviting groupthink. To defeat groupthink, a leader needs to take the opposite approach: to invite uncomfortable discussions and feedback, even when it challenges us as leaders. Unless we want groupthink, and the resulting poor decisions (which no one should ever want!), we must both encourage and engage our teams to push deeper, to think about what questions they aren't asking, to find a factor or series of factors that they haven't considered or that might be irreducibly important to making a better decision. Yes, the leader ultimately has to make the decision, but in this environment of psychological safety (as I detailed and discussed in chapter 2), even if the wrong decision ends up being made, it's a decision developed and delivered by the team, not in isolation by the "great man" or "great woman" at the head of the table. It's possible, of course, that a psychologically safe team can still deliver a bad decision, but a team of dunking ducks, swimming on a pond of groupthink, is much more likely to do so.

It's not about simply trying to move the team to the decision that the leader preconceived. It's about recognizing that the team should be all-in on the decision. Strong teams in a psychologically safe environment are committed to the decisions that result from their thoughtful deliberations, but in groupthinking, dunking ducks are only compliant and complicit with the will of the leader.

The team should be all-in, but if a mistake is made, a good leader owns the mistake and moves on. They don't make everybody on the team wear a poopy diaper.

I learned that when I was in team meetings, particularly when a decision was imminent, I needed to spend time with the team on things that really mattered, not things I could have read prior to the meeting. (Leaders are readers, and they focus on close fights and strategic horizons, after all.) As the leader who's ultimately responsible for the decision, it's my responsibility to prepare for the meeting in a way that encourages thoughtful input from the team and to guard and guide away from groupthink.

One example was detailed in chapter 4, where I described the discussions at the Air Force Academy about our vehicle in-service rate. You'll recall that, each month, my very capable chief logistician could happily report that we were well over the Air Force standard for the percentage of vehicles in service, with only 2.5 percent out of service. If we had stopped there and simply celebrated achievement beyond the standard, we might've missed an important detail that could have led to disaster. But by probing that statistic more deeply and asking, "What's in that other 2.5 percent?" we realized that we could be vulnerable to a commonly occurring wildfire if only two of our five firefighting vehicles were part of that small number of out-of-service vehicles. A team of groupthinking, leader-pleasing, praise-seeking, dunking ducks never would have come to such a realization.

* * *

Groupthink can be disastrous. To avoid it, leaders have to be very thoughtful about engaging considered contrarians in the conversation to help us make better decisions. We have to invite dissent, not squash it. We have to ask for and offer hard questions, even criticism, and not assume we have all the answers. When we see our team members ducking their heads, we need to recognize it's time to let them come up for air and contribute their thoughts. Leaders avoid a lot of problems when they commit to leading in this way.

Conclusion
Taking Off from Here

The illiterate of the twenty-first century
will not be those who cannot read or write
but those who cannot learn, unlearn, and relearn.

—Alvin Toffler

A career in leadership—military or civilian, government or private sector, for-profit or nonprofit—is indeed a wonderful journey. Professionals on that journey today, all over the world, are creating successes in ways the future leaders on their teams will certainly want to imitate.

I've had my share of opportunities over the years to learn, unlearn, and relearn the many things it takes to be an effective leader. I hope the exploration of these experiences throughout *The Mission of Leadership* has given you new ideas to incorporate into your own leadership tool kit and journey.

From finding your true north to honing your ability to lead to victory to overcoming and learning from the inevitable failures along the way, your own mission of leadership will share characteristics with mine, and with that of every other successful leader. But it will also be unique, unlike any other leader's journey.

I started by sharing how I came to join the Space Force in its early days and helped build that new service, guided by Polaris and purpose. As I was leaving the Air Force and retiring in December 2023, I reflected on the amazing blessing of being a part of the opportunity to do something really new: building the US Space Force to supercharge and surge space operations, not just for the United States but for our allies and partners around the world. I started to think about the things we're doing here in the twenty-first century and why those things matter not just to the people I served and supported in uniform but to anyone on a leadership journey. There were so many things I learned along the way.

Thank you for taking the time to read about some or all of the many things we covered in *The Mission of Leadership*. The contents of this book took a carefully curated career to build, but everything coalesced and connected in the time I spent helping to build the US Space Force. I know that experience made me a much better leader not only because I leaned in and learned but also because I believed in the utility and universality of the things we've talked about in this book. Every single one of these leadership truths was important to building the Space Force and doing it successfully.

On the last day I was serving in the Space Force, I sent a very short email to a couple hundred people—all the senior leaders, the chief human resources office team, and some of our downline teammates—because I wanted to share with them a few simple words about how important and impactful my time with them had been. I hoped they would take a couple of notes or nuggets from me that would help them continue building their own careers for however long they led and in whatever capacity, public or private.

I'm sharing that entire email with you (see appendix B) so you can see what was on my mind, which included many of the things we've discussed in *The Mission of Leadership*: the sturdy three-legged stool, the importance of having courage and leading boldly, teaching and trusting, moments that matter, and the importance of being word wise. I hope you'll see those truths reflected in that short email.

I've also shared the retirement speech I gave (appendix C) as I said my final farewell to public service (at least, as far as I could ascertain at that time—who knows where the future will take any of us?). Again, you'll catch glimpses of the material from all thirteen chapters of *The Mission of Leadership* in that speech and see how these concepts informed and instructed me as a leader across the arc of my career. I definitely included some discussion of my family, which is incredibly important to me, but I also discussed leadership traits included in this book, and I hope you'll see what you've been reading about come to life.

Mine was a "stripes to stars" journey—from the stripes I wore on my sleeve as a young enlisted man planning to merely put in my four years to the General Officer stars I wore on my shoulder boards at the end of an unbelievable and unexpected thirty-year leadership journey. I hope you'll agree that the ideas presented in *The Mission of Leadership* are impactful, important, and insightful to our organizations and to the people we lead, now more than ever.

* * *

As I continue my leadership journey as a consultant, confidant, collaborator, and coach, I would be happy to help you with your own wonderful leadership mission. If you would like an experienced travel companion as you launch your leadership career into the next "wild blue yonder," please reach out for a consultation.

Shawn@themissionofleadership.com

APPENDIX A
CAMPBELL'S CUTS

These were mentioned in chapter 1, "All Thrust, No Vector." This specific list is what I shared with my US Transportation Command team when I became chief human capital officer in July 2016. It's a good representative sample of my quick way of sharing my leadership philosophy and my key focus areas no matter our organizational objectives. These views anchored my leadership roles and responsibilities for many years.

- Readiness is Job 1
- Be worthy every day
- Catch people doing things well/right
- Show up, work hard, don't quit
- Invest in people
- Never be afraid to do what is right

- No one can take your reputation, but you can give it away
- Words matter
- Vision only works when you're looking up and out
- Learn constantly
- Leaders are readers
- Watch personal and team gas gauges
- Be a fire preventer, not just a firefighter
- Break things . . . fail falling forward
- Commitment + Compliance = Mission Success
- "US"

APPENDIX B
SPACE FORCE FAREWELL

The following is the text of the email I sent on December 20, 2021, to about two hundred Space Force leaders (including General Raymond, who wrote the forward for this book), at the end of my tenure as the first-ever deputy chief human capital officer for the US Space Force and prior to returning to the Air Force for my final assignment before retiring.

Leaders and Teammates,

I've had some time to remember and reflect on the past twenty-plus months and am sharing a few thoughts.

What a remarkable journey this has been. Certainly it hasn't always been easy or fun; but we have been making, and continue to make, history together.

When I got the call in January 2020 to ask if I'd join the team, I had no inkling, information, or insight into just what would unfold in the days, weeks, and months following.

I've shared the story with some of you that while my first official day with this team wasn't until May 1, 2020, unsurprisingly, the calling necessitated working Space Force–related things well in advance of that date.

My first decision brief to the Vice Chief of Space Operations was in April 2020. That proved foundationally fortuitous as that briefing sought his approval of the framework we developed to build our Human Capital Strategy, now the Guardian Ideal. It also sought and secured funding to partner with Gartner as we developed, and now delivered (and made publicly available), the Guardian Ideal.

Our team has grown tenfold since those early days, and I've seen us grow in confidence, capability, and connection.

We energized and engaged in doing something irreducibly important to our national security, something that no one has done in seven decades and for which no off-the-shelf plan or playbook exists.

Every day is seemingly filled with another "first": another opportunity, another challenge, and another milestone achieved. How is that possible?

I find the answer in one word . . . *character*. I think a quote often attributed to the American novelist James Lane Allen captures this well: "Adversity does not build character, it reveals it." And what marvelous and motivated character has been revealed.

I've heard it said, "You are the five people with whom you most spend time." If that's true, and I think it is, I was glad to have spent this time with you.

Over the next couple weeks as we gather near family and friends to celebrate this time of year, I encourage you to take a few minutes to think about how much you have given, and gained, being a part of this team.

Thank you for making me better by your example and allowing me to be a part of this effort. It's been a pure privilege and a humble honor to have served alongside you these near two years.

Semper Supra!

With deep admiration and appreciation,
Brigadier General Shawn Campbell

APPENDIX C
AIR FORCE RETIREMENT SPEECH

This is the text of the farewell speech I delivered, yes, without notes, at my retirement ceremony on November 10, 2023, at George Washington's home and my favorite place in the Washington, DC, area, the historic Mount Vernon.

OPENING

Duty, honor, country. During his famous farewell address to the cadets at West Point on May 12, 1962, General Douglas MacArthur time and again came back to these three words: *duty*, *honor*, *country*. These words undergird the core and the character of the leaders we have been developing at West Point since 1802, and although these words were not ensconced and enshrined as their motto until 1898, the year prior to when MacArthur entered there as a cadet, the cadets and classes from the very beginning embodied, embraced, and exemplified them.

On what is known as The Plain, the historic parade field at the oldest of our military academies, MacArthur, then eighty-two years old, delivered what is considered by many military historians as the greatest speech ever spoken by any one of our nation's foremost and formidable flag officers. His words were at once both powerful and prescient.

He spoke of the coming space age, the changing national and international landscapes, and how the nature of war would evolve in the coming decades. He was seeing a future that many could have only imagined. Perhaps and probably, his fifty years of learning and leadership on the world stage afforded him a sight-filled and sober understanding of what would be because he had lived through what was for so long.

Ladies and gentlemen, good morning. Thank you for being here to share in these moments and in this milestone with my family and me. We are at once amazed and appreciative of you taking the time to be here, both those in person and those watching online. We want to acknowledge the great lengths to which many of you went to be here in person today. Family and friends have traveled from far and wide, from Alaska, Washington, California, Texas, Colorado, Missouri, Illinois, Florida, North Carolina, South Carolina, New York, and across Virginia and the national capital region. Online, people are similarly watching from across our fruited plain, and even a few from overseas locations. There are people here and online who have been a part of my life from day one, including someone from nearly every one of my career assignments.

You may wonder why I opened with notes from MacArthur. After all, he was a soldier, not an airman. As I reflected on the thirty years we consider today, I note that when I left for basic enlisted military training, I did so leaving Beth and my immediate family from MacArthur's mother's hometown of Norfolk, Virginia. And, as we depart company here, I will return and retire, at least for a time, back to Norfolk, where MacArthur and his second wife Jean are buried. There are other things connecting him and me; for example, he served as West Point's superintendent, and I served as senior leader at the Air Force Academy, both of us serving and supporting the growth and development of military leaders of character. My service and career do not merit being named in the history books as MacArthur is, but his farewell words have resonated with me as a history student for many years now.

This is my farewell address, closing out what may very well be the end of my public service career. Rather than reuse "Duty, honor, and country," which I cannot do with MacArthur's vision, voice, and vibrance, we transpose those words into three that aptly apply to my military career: service, sacrifice, and sunrise.

SERVICE

Writing to Benedict Arnold in September 1775, George Washington, on whose home grounds we're gathered this morning, wrote about the value of service: "Every post is honorable in which a man can serve his country." This sentiment was challenged many times during the next eight years as we fought for and secured our national independence. Arnold betrayed his service, and Washington, at West Point, where he had been dispatched to defend the high grounds there.

Later still, following the British surrender at Yorktown on October 19, 1781, and months prior to the Paris Treaty signing officially ending our Revolutionary War, the Continental Army became purposeless and encamped at Newburgh, New York, just north of West Point. There was growing discontent, especially among the officers, that they may not be compensated either for their current service or with the pensions they had been promised during the war.

What is known as the Newburgh conspiracy was hatched. The effort was to pressure the Continental Congress into pledging and promising payments, now and in the future. On Saturday, March 15, 1783, General George Washington sought to put an end to the conspiracy. The officers assembled in the Temple of Virtue, the meeting hall for officers at that encampment, to discuss their plan, and Washington unexpectedly arrived to address them.

His address is now legend. His presence and powerful prose turned the conspiracy asunder largely based on his own example, and his personal appeal to the assembled, that service itself was the virtue of the moment. He implored the officers to think about all they had accomplished and not to sully their reputations or their honor with such a conspiracy at what would be the end of most of their military careers. Service was the virtue of the moment. I think it still is.

Thinking back across the long years of my service, it did not start with a sense of national pride, desire for honor, or a sense of obligation to this country, which has given me so much more than I could have asked. No, like many within the sound of my voice, I simply and solely joined the Air Force as a means to an end. A way, as many of you have heard me share previously, to finish paying for college. I was planning to learn a skill, earn the GI Bill, and return home after my four-year contract to Norfolk and to Old Dominion University to finish my studies. All along the way, my family and I have been beautifully blessed by purpose, people, and promise: The purpose to seek the security and safety of all we hold so dear, surrounded by people committed to the same shared goals, and the promise of a fulfilling and richly rewarding career.

No matter who you are, where you're from, what circumstances you've had to overcome, or what you do, officer, enlisted, and civilian alike, here in service to our country, you will find purpose, people, and promise worth pursuing. This is why my family and I have served for the past thirty years.

When we seek a life of service, we quickly recognize and realize it is impossible without sacrifice.

SACRIFICE

MacArthur, quoting the great Greek philosopher Plato in that farewell address, shared, "Only the dead have seen the last of war." My service and sacrifice started after Desert Shield and Desert Storm were done. The decade in which I enlisted was part of what we call the Peace Dividend. The Soviet Union was long gone, Saddam Hussein and Iraq's military capabilities were shells of their former selves, our nation was alone as the world's only superpower, and second place wasn't even close. Into this era of peace and prosperity, my career really took off. Mr. Horace "HL" Larry (who officiated my retirement ceremony and is a general officer equivalent) spoke wonderfully about that, making me sound much better than I really am.

Life was good. Beth and I had both finished college, I was now a young officer, and we were growing our family, bringing Taylor and Carter into the world. For eight years, there was little service sacrifice, especially when compared to what the next two decades would deliver and demand. Like many, if not most, joining us this morning, what we simply refer to as 9/11 happened, and the world changed.

Beth and I had just returned to our walk-up apartment on Spangdahlem Air Base in Germany, from a medical appointment at Landstuhl Regional Medical Center an hour-plus away. I was in our bedroom when Beth called to me from the living room to see what was on the television. It was mid-afternoon for us, mid-morning here on the East Coast. The next moments changed all our lives forever.

A few weeks later, like so many others, I deployed. I left for Incirlik Air Base in Turkey to become, essentially, the commander of the Hodja Village Tent City, where in the space of weeks after I arrived in early November, we more than doubled the population from 1,200 to more than 2,400 personnel. We supported Operations Northern Watch over Iraq and Enduring Freedom in Afghanistan and supported the unnamed operation moving Taliban prisoners from Afghanistan to Guantanamo Bay. It was just the start of enormous sacrifices we'd pay as a family. Starting then, and across the next twenty-two years, we have all sacrificed.

I have missed so very much in the lives of my wife and children. This is not a badge of honor, because the sacrifice is not mine alone. Beth and I have moved to new assignment locations twelve times and lived in seventeen different homes. We moved homes within assignment locations several times. Taylor and Carter experienced most of those same assignments and home moves. Not all, but most. Those are sacrifices. They have sacrificed significantly.

Over the course of my career, I have been on temporary duty trips well north of two hundred times, forty-eight times in just the past few years alone. I think I have more flight time than some of our pilots. Those were as short as one day, and as long as ten weeks. Along the way, two deployments, a one-year remote assignment, and the last four and half years living apart from Beth, Taylor, and Carter, not to mention the too many days, weeks, months, and years I worked many more hours than I probably should have. In all, I calculate

Beth and I have been apart for the better part of nine years while I've also been away from Taylor for seven and Carter for six. Modern technology helped collapse the gaps some, but it is foolishness not to know the sacrifice we all made.

I think of these sacrifices as time, tests, and triumphs. Obviously thirty years is time, and a lot of it. Some days, it seems it cannot have been that long; other days, well, I feel every bit of those decades pulling myself together in the morning.

There were tests for all of us along the way, but today, as evidenced here, the family I started with remains. It was not always easy, or fun, or simple; but because of who Beth is, our family remains intact. Her sacrifices were, very likely, so much greater than my own. It's easier for the serving members because we plug right into a team. The family has to start all over, every time. That is not lost on me.

The triumphs were manifold and magnificent in reflection. Here, I don't mean awards or accolades won, or the reward of rank; rather, I mean the fullness of life spent doing something worthwhile, and along the way seeing both Taylor and Carter grow into very fine young adults—well educated, well adjusted—and doing so across all those moves and sacrifices.

Now, ladies and gentlemen, please indulge me for a couple minutes as Beth and I thank Taylor and Carter for the sacrifices they made and for living a life they did not seek as I served. Kiddos, please join me on stage. We have a presentation for you, the military kids medal, denoting the importance of your service and sacrifice, and how that supported me and your mom across your entire lives to this point.

When General Washington concluded his written remarks, quashing the Newburgh conspiracy, he ended by reading a letter from Virginia Congressman Joseph Jones supporting the officers' pay demands. It's unclear whether he meant to stumble and stammer at first, but it has been established that he used the imagery of what he did prior to reading to secure and solidify the outcome he desired. While reaching into his pocket to retrieve a pair of glasses to read that letter, he remarked, "Gentlemen, you must pardon me. I have grown gray in your service and now find myself growing blind." That incident was so moving, many of the assembled wept because Washington so embodied excellence, energy, and endurance. They had never seen him wearing glasses.

So, as I reach into my own pocket for my glasses to read these citations, I really knew it was time for me to retire, aside from my graying temples, when in the same week, on consecutive days, a Tuesday and a Wednesday, I ordered both bifocals and hearing aids.

[Here I read the kids' medal citation and presented the framed items to my children.]

I have Beth's military wife medal also framed for presentation. Because of who she is, she wanted the focus to be on Taylor and Carter.

Where, then, do all these years of service and sacrifice leave us? They lead to the sunrise of a new era.

SUNRISE

Given we are here, on these historic grounds, a favorite location for my family and me, it is fitting we return one last time to our nation's sunrise to consider one more historic story. During the three months of the Constitutional Convention, over which then-retired General Washington presided, he sat in a chair made in 1779 by John Folwell. It is known to us as the Rising Sun Armchair. Inlaid at the top of the chair back, where Washington's head would have rested, is a shimmering sun. Benjamin Franklin, as captured by James Madison in the record, was puzzling aloud over whether that sun was rising or setting.

He concluded it was in fact rising, just as our nation was rising out of years of struggle and strife, seeking to get out from under British colonial rule and chart our own course as a free and independent nation. My family and I look upon today in much the same manner. While this is my military farewell, this is by no means, at least I hope and pray, a near precursor to my life's final sunrise. Rather, it's the rising of new opportunities, openings, and, yes, likely obstacles.

I do not know, of course, how many more sunrises God will grant me. What I do know is that tomorrow we will see yet another great and glorious sunrise, the dawning of a new day with all its opportunities, openings, and obstacles to overcome alongside new purpose, people, and promise.

A few know already, but I can now share in complete openness, come January 2024, I am pleased to be starting as a human resources executive partner at Gartner Incorporated. Other opportunities and openings have also presented themselves, such as performing both paid and unpaid board work, developing leaders, and finally getting paid for giving speeches. I look forward to doing all of this under this next sunrise as well.

CLOSING

We shall close where we began, hearing once more from General MacArthur on The Plain and his final charge to the cadets on that marvelous May morning because those words resound, resonate, and ring in my ears, and that's not my tinnitus.

MacArthur said, "You are the leaven which binds together the entire fabric of our national system of defense. From your ranks come the great captains who hold the nation's destiny in their hands the moment the war tocsin sounds. The long gray line has never failed us. Were you to do so, a million ghosts in olive drab, in brown khaki, in blue and gray, would rise from their white crosses, thundering those magic words—*duty, honor, country.*"

As this era of my family's and my service and sacrifice sunsets and we awake awash in a new sunrise, his charge is my channeled charge to those officers, enlisted, and civilians still serving and sacrificing for the safety and security of our nation because my part of it, at least wearing the uniform, has come to a close.

Ten years ago, almost to the day of this ceremony, on November 9, 2013, my family buried my grandfather Stevenson. He was a proud World War II Navy veteran, serving from 1942 to 1945 in both the Atlantic and Pacific theaters. We buried him in his Navy uniform. During his celebration of life service, I said to him, and to the assembled, that his watch was now over. He is relieved and I have the watch. Fair winds and following seas, faithful servant sailor.

Today, I cede the watch. It has been the honor of a lifetime to serve with and for you, standing shoulder to shoulder, sometimes bended knee to bended knee—and as we remember and reflect on those we lost along the way, sometimes bowed head to bowed head—but always as brothers and sisters in arms.

Ladies and gentlemen, I stand relieved. Thank you.

About the Author

SHAWN CAMPBELL is a retired United States Air Force Brigadier General with more than thirty years of experience, education, and expertise leading organizations and developing teams in high-stakes and high-demand environments across the globe. He culminated his distinguished military career as the director of Air Force Manpower, Organizations, and Resources, where he was responsible for leading the management and oversight of the Air Force's personnel enterprise encompassing more than 694,000 military and civilian members and the programming of more than $64 billion in annual funding for the personnel pay portion of the Air Force's budget. He also set standards and policy for strategic personnel sourcing, performance management, organizational structure, and manpower data systems.

He served in a wide variety of positions of ever-increasing responsibility levels, including leading the three-thousand-person air base wing at the United States Air Force Academy. Essentially, he served as the Academy's mayor, directly supporting the deliberate development of future Air Force leaders. He is a deeply experienced human resources professional and C-suite-level executive.

In January 2020, Shawn was hand-selected by the Department of the Air Force to serve as the first-ever deputy chief human capital officer for the newly forming United States Space Force. He was part of the initial leadership team that created the newest United States military service in more than seventy years. Known for delivering impacting and innovative talent management initiatives, he was tasked, among other strategic priorities, to develop and deliver the Space Force's first-ever talent management strategy.

Shawn's purpose and passion are to help others and organizations best educate themselves to reach and realize improved outcomes; elevate connections to serve and support teammates reaching their full potential and becoming the best versions of themselves; and extend individual and organizational capabilities, capacities, and competencies that drive and deliver world-class professional and personal performance.

Shawn holds both a bachelor's and a master's degree in business administration and a graduate certificate in organizational management. He served as an Air Force strategic policy intern at the Pentagon and was a national security fellow at the Kennedy School of Government, Harvard University. Shawn also serves on the governing board of advisors for a nonprofit public media organization.

www.ingramcontent.com/pod-product-compliance
Lightning Source LLC
Chambersburg PA
CBHW022040210326
41458CB00088B/6887/J